The
Writer's
Book
Of
Quotes

Rocky Henriques

compiler

ISBN-13: 978-1981254781

ISBN-10: 1981254781

Carpenter's Corner Press,
Utica, Mississippi

The quoted ideas expressed in this book are not, in all cases, exact quotations, as some have been edited for clarity and brevity. In all cases, the author has attempted to maintain the writer's original intent. In many cases, quoted material for this book was obtained from secondary sources. While every effort was made to ensure the accuracy of these sources, the accuracy cannot be guaranteed. For additions, deletions, corrections or clarifications in future editions of this text, please contact the compiler.

*For
Emma Claire
and
Joshua*

Contents

Foreword

One particular young author stood out in my mind while I was compiling and arranging these thoughts. My granddaughter Emma Claire has ventured into the world of creative writing, and it is my hope and prayer that this little book will encourage her and her little brother Joshua to write and keep writing, even if only for themselves. So this foreword takes the form of a letter to those precious youngsters, even if they won't fully appreciate the wisdom of these quotations for a few years. You're welcome to look over my shoulder as I write to them:

My dear Emma Claire and Joshua,

I first began collecting quotations to fulfill a requirement for a speech class assignment when I was a junior in high school. We were to look for poems and quotations which could be used in speeches, and keep them in a notebook. That assignment quickly became an obsession, and I have been collecting the wise, thought-provoking and sometimes witty words of others ever since. Entire shelves in my personal library are packed with books of quotations. And I still have that original notebook.

Once I discovered quotations they were suddenly appearing everywhere. I noticed them in sidebars in magazines, in footnotes, in speeches and books. That's when I began using pens and highlighters. In those low-tech days the counselor in my high school hung a chalkboard overhead in the hallway, and every day he would climb a ladder to write motivational words for us to think about as we entered the building. Some of the cooler kids made light of those words, but I was fascinated. They looked every day so they could mock; I locked my eyes on that chalkboard suspended from the ceiling to collect one more quotation.

It occurred to me one day that there should be a collection of advice various authors have given about their craft. There may be other books similar to this one; I am not claiming this is an original idea. This is merely a collection of some of the quotations which have inspired me, and they appear here to encourage you or some other aspiring writer, young or old. Perhaps you will find thoughts on writing from authors you have known and loved many years, or you may discover a new author you've never heard of. Hopefully, you will keep this book handy, in print or digital format, and turn to it over and over for inspiration and help.

As you read, you will discover in some cases opinions which are opposite to one another. One author says this, another says that. Their opposing viewpoints are included only to show that these are merely opinions and not law.

For example, one writer has said that he never revises as he writes, while another says he always does. This author doesn't believe there is such a thing as writer's block, while that one offers suggestions on how to overcome it. And that's perfectly okay. What is powerful for one doesn't work at all for someone else. I hope you will learn that you must forge your own path and figure it out for yourself, that you don't necessarily have to do it the way someone else does. You don't have to write in the same style, or about the same subjects, or at the same times. You simply must be yourself. It's certainly okay to learn from others, even try to imitate their styles, but above all else, be yourself.

So curl up somewhere in a quiet place and drink deeply of the wisdom and experience of these authors who have shared their thoughts with the world.

And I hope you will remember that your Papaw put this together with great love for you.

1
Who Is A Writer?

A writer is someone for whom
writing is more difficult than it is
for other people.

Thomas Mann

Real writers are those who want to
write, need to write, have to write.

Robert Penn Warren

You either have to write or you shouldn't be writing. That's all.

Joss Whedon

A writer is a writer not because she writes well and easily, because she has amazing talent, or because everything she does is golden. A writer is a writer because, even when there is no hope, even when nothing you do shows any sign of promise, you keep writing anyway.

Junot Diaz

A writer is someone who has taught his mind to misbehave.

Oscar Wilde

The thing that defines a writer is that the writer writes.

Chuck Wendig

Writing is a calling, not a choice.

Isabel Allende

You must learn to be three people at once: writer, character and reader.

Nancy Kress

A person is a fool to become a writer. His only compensation is absolute freedom. He has no master except his own soul, and that, I am sure, is why he does it.

Roald Dahl

Write like it matters, and it will.

Libba Bray

Being a writer requires an intoxication with language.

Jim Harrison

Growing up I believed only certain people were allowed to write books—namely, fancy literary heirs who had gone to the right school and university. Not people like me. But of course, anyone can write a book. And anyone should, so that we have more diversity of voices in publishing.

Julie Mayhew

The only writer to whom you should compare yourself is the writer you were yesterday.

David B. Schlosser

Being a writer was never a choice. It was an irresistible compulsion.

Walter Jon Williams

And although it is sometimes easy to forget,

wanting to be a writer is not about reviews or advances or how many copies are printed or sold. It is much simpler than that, and much more passionate. If you do it right, and if they publish it, you may actually leave something behind that can last forever.

Alice Hoffman

Each of us is a book waiting to be written.

Thomas M. Cirignano

I think you must remember that a writer is a simple-minded person to begin with and go on that basis. He's not a great mind, he's not a great thinker, he's not a philosopher. He's a storyteller.

Erskine Caldwell

The role of a writer is not to say what we all can say, but what we are unable to say.

Anaïs Nin

You are a writer the moment you start writing, not when you've sold your first book.

Rob Bignell

Every secret of a writer's soul, every

experience of his life, every quality of his mind, is written large in his works.

Virginia Woolf

Every author, however modest, keeps a most outrageous vanity chained like a madman in the padded cell of his breast.

Logan Pearsall Smith

No one is born a writer. You must become a writer. In fact, you never cease becoming, because you never stop learning how to write. Even now, I am becoming a writer. And so are you.

Joe Bunting

The first person you should think of pleasing, in writing a book, is yourself. If you can amuse yourself for the length of time it takes to write a book, the publisher and the readers can and will come later.

Patricia Highsmith

A writer is a person who cares what words mean, what they say, how they say it. Writers know words are their way towards truth and freedom, and so they use them with care, with thought, with fear, with delight. By using words well they strengthen their souls. Storytellers and poets spend their lives learning that skill and art of using words well. And their words make the souls of their readers stronger, brighter, deeper.

Ursula K. Le Guin

You need a certain amount of nerve to be a writer.

Margaret Atwood

A writer is a world trapped in a person.

Victor Hugo

A writer is someone who spends years patiently trying to discover the second being inside him.

Orhan Pamuk

A writer is a writer because even when there is no hope, even when nothing you do shows any sign of promise, you keep writing anyway.

Junot Diaz

If you want to be a writer, write. Write and write and write. If you stop, start again. Save everything that you write. If you feel blocked, write through it until you feel your creative juices flowing again. Write. Writing is what makes a writer, nothing more and nothing less.

Anne Rice

The job of a writer is not to convey emotion, but to invoke it.

Eric T. Benoit

A writer is simply a photographer of thoughts.

Brandon A. Trean

Writers open our hearts and minds, and give us maps to our own selves.

Alain de Botton

As a writer, you get to play, you get to alter time, you get to come up with the smart lines and the clever comebacks you wish you'd thought of.

Iain Banks

My experience is that there are people who, perhaps vaguely, like the idea of being writers, and then there are actual writers. The difference between these two groups is that the former can take it or leave it, depending on various circumstances; whereas the latter have no option but to write.

Adam Roberts

Never take a writer for granted. They are snipers armed with words. They know how to aim with sentences, how to fire with paragraphs, and how to immortalize their kills in verse.

Nikita Gall

What makes someone want to be a writer? Clearly, one thing this dream requires is a ferocious hunger, a hunger for recognition, a yearning to be heard that roars through the soul with a sound so great that the stories often feel as if they are discovered rather than invented.

Susan Cheever

If you can quit, then quit. If you can't quit, you're a writer.

R. A. Salvatore

Many people hear voices when no one is there. Some of them are called "mad" and are shut up in rooms where they stare at the walls every day. Others are called "writers" and they do pretty much the same thing.

Ray Bradbury

Maybe you have to be a little crazy to write a

good and original book.

Patricia Gauch

I am a writer. Therefore, I am not sane.

Edgar Allan Poe

2
Why Should You Write?

I write because I can't not write …
If I have an idea circling in my brain
and can't get it, it begins to poison my
waking existence, until I'm unable
to function in polite company
or even hold a simple conversation.

Jodi Picoult

You don't write because
you want to say something.
You write because you
have something to say.

F. Scott Fitzgerald

I write to give myself strength. I write to be the characters that I am not. I write to explore all the things I'm afraid of.

Joss Whedon

Write to write. Write because you need to write. Write to settle the rage within you. Write with internal purpose. Write about something or someone that means so much to you, that you don't care what others think.

Nick Miller

I write because I must. It's not a choice or a pastime, it's an unyielding calling and my passion.

Elizabeth Reyes

If you want to change the world, pick up your pen and write.

Martin Luther

I want to write books that unlock the traffic jam in everybody's head.

John Updike

If you do not breathe through writing, if you do not cry out in writing, or sing in writing,

then don't write, because our culture has no
use for it.

Anaïs Nin

If you don't see the book you want on the
shelf, write it.

Beverly Cleary

My morning begins with trying not to get up
before the sun rises. But when I do, it's
because my head is too full of words, and I
just need to get to my desk and start dumping
them into a file. I always wake with sentences
pouring into my head.

Barbara Kingsolver

We write to taste life twice.

Anaïs Nin

Writing stories is my escape from the
claustrophobia of individuality. It lets me, at
least for a while, live more than one life, walk
more than one path. Reading, of course, can
do the same.

Emma Donoghue

Why does one begin to write? Because she
feels misunderstood, I guess. Because it never
comes out clearly enough when she tries to

speak. Because she wants to rephrase the world, to take it in and give it back again differently, so that everything is used and nothing is lost. Because it's something to do to pass the time until she is old enough to experience the things she writes about.

Nicole Krauss

Writing is medicine. It is an appropriate antidote to injury. It is an appropriate companion for any difficult change.

Julia Cameron

There were times when I was afraid I would never sell another book, but I never doubted I'd write another book.

George R. R. Martin

If I don't write to empty my mind, I go mad.

Lord Byron

Why write? Why should we all write? This is what I recommend: purchase a small notebook. Post-its. Colorful pages. Plain paper. Hold a pen. Pick a word and see where that word takes you. Because you store everything in your body: the gorgeous, the ugly, the painful, the ecstatic. It's all there locked away in your cells where memory, tension and confusion remain day after day, waiting to be set free. You don't have to show it to an audience or your spouse or your children or even yourself again.

But when it's written down as a list, as a paragraph or poem or story, you can go to bed with a greater understanding of yourself, of the world, or even of both: yourself in this world. And at the very least, you know all those things are out of your body. Writing is essentially becoming free. It all begins with a word.

Victoria Erickson

Writing is the best way to talk without being interrupted.

Jules Renard

When I sit down to write a book, I do not say to myself, "I am going to produce a work of art." I write it because there is some lie that I want to expose, some fact to which I want to draw attention, and my initial concern is to get a hearing.

George Orwell

I hope that someday when I am gone, someone, somewhere, picks my soul up off these pages and thinks, "I would have loved her."

Nicole Lyons

When I don't write, I feel my world shrinking. I feel I am in a prison. I feel I lose my fire and my color. It should be a necessity, as the sea needs to heaven, and I call it breathing.

Anaïs Nin

To me, the greatest pleasure of writing is not what it's about, but the music the words make.

Truman Capote

To write well about the elegant world you have to know it and experience it to the depths of your being ... what matters is not whether you love it or hate it, but only to be quite clear about your position regarding it.

Italo Calvino

Writing begins from a rant, but it doesn't end there. You write until the writing brings you to a place of light. You have to travel through the rant to the light ... When I was younger I did a lot of ranting. But ranting is uncomposted writing. No one wants to accept the coffee grounds and the banana peels, but they will pick up the flower. We have to learn to write with love, until the light shines through.

Sandra Cisneros

Writing is a form of therapy; sometimes I wonder how all those who do not write, compose or paint can manage to escape the madness, melancholia, the panic and fear which is inherent in a human situation.

Graham Greene

The writer must believe that what he is doing is the most important thing in the world. And he must hold to his illusion even if he knows it is not true.

John Steinbeck

A person is a fool to become a writer. His only compensation is absolute freedom. He has no master except his own soul, and that, I am sure, is why he does it.

Roald Dahl

If you have any young friends who aspire to become writers, the second greatest favor you can do them is to present them with copies of The Elements of Style. The first greatest, of course, is to shoot them now, while they're happy.

Dorothy Parker

Move the reader, make them happy and sad and excited and scared. Make them stare into space after they've put the book down, thinking about the tale that's become a part of them.

James Dashner

Words are things, and a small drop of ink, falling like dew upon a thought, produces that which makes thousands, perhaps millions, think.

Lord Byron

Words are sacred. They deserve respect. If you get the right ones, in the right order, you can nudge the world a little.

Tom Stoppard

A good poem is a contribution to reality. The world is never the same once a good poem has been added to it. A good poem helps to change the shape of the universe, helps to extend everyone's knowledge of himself and the world around him.

Dylan Thomas

I choose to write because it's perfect for me. It's an escape, a place I can go to hide. It's a friend, when I feel out casted from everyone else. It's a journal, when the only story I can tell is my own. It's a book, when I need to be somewhere else. It's control, when I feel so out of control. It's healing, when everything seems pretty messed up. And it's fun, when life is just flat-out boring.

Alysha Speer

You should write because you love the shape of stories and sentences and the creation of different worlds on a page.

Annie Proulx

I'm just going to write because I cannot help it.

Charlotte Bronte

You have the itch for writing born in you. It's quite incurable. What are you going to do with it?

L. M. Montgomery

A day in which I don't write leaves a taste of ashes.

Simone de Beauvoir

Because when I write, it's more than just me at a keyboard. It's the universe converging within the pandemonium of my mind, and turning it into something beautiful.

Lyndsey Evenstar

I write to become someone else, that better, smarter self that lives inside my dumbstruck twin. I write to invite the voices in, to watch the angel wrestle, to feel the devil gather on its haunches and rise. I write to hear myself breathing. I write to be doing something while I wait to be called to my appointment with death. I write to be done writing.

Dorianne Laux

Never forget that writing is as close as we get to keeping a hold on the thousand and one things—childhood, certainties, cities, doubts, dreams, instants, phrases, parents, loves—that go on slipping, like sand, through our fingers.

Salman Rushdie

I write to give myself strength. I write to be the characters that I am not. I write to explore all the things I'm afraid of.

Joss Whedon

Writing is also a tool you can use your whole life: to help people, make them laugh, change their minds. You can do it for people in faraway countries, even for people who haven't been born yet. Writing is a way to live forever.

Barbara Kingsolver

I just knew there were stories I wanted to tell.

Octavia E. Butler

I believe one writes because one has to create a world in which one can live. I had to create a world of my own, like a climate, a country, an atmosphere in which I could breathe, reign, and recreate myself when destroyed by living. That, I believe, is the reason for every work of art.

Anais Nin

You ask me why I spend my life writing? Do I find entertainment? Is it worthwhile? Above all, does it pay? If not, then, is there a reason? I write only because there is a voice within me. That will not be stilled.

Sylvia Plath

There are many good reasons for writing that
have nothing to do with being published.
Writing is a powerful search mechanism, and
one of its satisfactions is that it allows you to
come to terms with your life narrative. It also
allows you to work through some of life's
hardest knocks—loss, grief, illness, addiction,
disappointment, failure—and to find
understanding and solace.

William Zinsser

The role of a writer is not to say what we all
can say,
but what we are unable to say.

Anais Nin

Learning to write, is learning to think. You
don't know anything clearly, if you can't state
it in writing.

S.I. Hayakawa

I write because I don't know what I think
until I read what I say.

Flannery O'Connor

I do not sit down at my desk to put into verse something that is already clear in my mind. If it were clear in my mind, I should have no incentive or need to write about it. We do not write in order to be understood; we write in order to understand.

C. S. Lewis

Writing is how I understand everything that happens. Writing is the only way I know to move on.

Delia Ephron

Why do writers write? Because it isn't there.

Thomas Berger

I think you should write for yourself, for the joy of it, the pleasure of it, and for the satisfaction that you have in learning about your life.

Peter Taylor

I only write for myself. I write the book I want to read, the book that I miss.

Ann Patchett

Writing provides a way to make sense, in language, of the puzzling, wild, beautiful moments our lives keep delivering to us.

Joy Castro

Writing a book is a horrible, exhausting struggle, like a long bout of some painful illness. One would never undertake such a thing if one were not driven on by some demon whom one can neither resist nor understand.

George Orwell

I write entirely to find out what I'm thinking, what I'm looking at, what I see and what it means. What I want and what I fear.

Joan Dixon

There is no greater agony than bearing an untold story inside you.

Maya Angelou

The act of putting pen to paper encourages pause for thought, this in turn makes us think more deeply about life, which helps us regain our equilibrium.

Norbet Platt

I can shake off everything as I write; my

sorrows disappear, my courage is reborn.

Anne Frank

When you speak, your words echo across the room. When you write, your words echo across the ages.

Bud Gardner

3

Writers Should Read

I am always chilled and astonished by
the would-be writers who ask me for
advice and admit, quite blithely, that
they "don't have time to read." This is
like a guy starting up Mount Everest
saying that he didn't have time to buy
any rope or pitons.

Stephen King

Read a thousand books
and your words will flow like a river.

Virginia Woolf

Just as composers go to concerts
and artists go to galleries, writers read.

Judith Barrington

The greatest part of a writer's time is spent in reading in order to write. A man will turn over half a library to make a book.

Samuel Johnson

Learning to write sound, interesting, sometimes elegant prose is the work of a lifetime. The only way I know to do it is to read a vast deal of the best writing available, prose and poetry, with keen attention, and find a way to make use of this reading in one's own writing. The first step is to become a slow reader.

Joseph Epstein

Just write every day of your life. Read intensely. Then see what happens. Most of my friends who are put on that diet have very pleasant careers.

Ray Bradbury

We write by the light of every story we have ever read.

Richard Peck

If you don't have the time to read, you don't

have the time or the tools to write.

Stephen King

Writing and reading decrease our sense of isolation. They deepen and widen and expand our sense of life: they feed the soul.

Anne Lamott

Indeed, learning to write may be part of learning to read. For all I know, writing comes out of a superior devotion to reading.

Eudora Welty

Writing comes from reading, and reading is the finest teacher of how to write.

Annie Proulx

I don't know whether I could do either one, reading or writing, without the other.

Eudora Welty

Read. If you read, you not only expand your vision and understanding of life, but will sooner or later bump into writers whose work will help mold your own. Not dictate it— mold it.

Jonathan Carroll

Read! Read! Read! It's vital to fill that well of

creativity within you. Otherwise you'll simply run out of words and ideas. By reading other authors' books, you'll learn what works, what doesn't, absorb new words, trigger new ideas, and above all immerse yourself in the world of writing. A writer who doesn't read can never be an author!

Chris Bradford

Read, read, read, never stop reading. And when you can't read anymore … write.

James Baldwin

Read, read, read. Read everything—trash, classics, good and bad, and see how they do it. Just like a carpenter who works as an apprentice and studies the master. Read! You'll absorb it. Then write. If it is good, you'll find out. If it's not, throw it out the window.

William Faulkner

Keep writing. Learn your craft … and read, read read.

Lurlene McDaniel

If you want to be a writer you must do two

things above all others: read a lot, and write a lot.

Stephen King

For all I know, writing comes out of a superior devotion to reading.

Eudora Welty

You need to read. You can't be a writer if you're not a reader. It's the great writers who teach us how to write.

Madeleine L'Engle

Writing is only reading turned inside out.

John Updike

The greatest part of a writer's time is spent in reading in order to write. A man will turn over half a library to make a book.

Samuel Johnson

Writing is learned by imitation. If anyone asked me how I learned to write, I'd say I learned by reading the men and women who were doing the kind of writing I wanted to do and trying to figure out how they did it.

William Zinsser

Read widely and with discrimination. Bad writing is contagious.

P. D. James

We write in response to what we read and learn; and in the end we write out of our deepest selves, the live, breathing, bleeding place where the pictures form, and where it all begins.

Andrea Barrett

Don't go reading the latest prizewinners and bestsellers in the hope of discovering what publishers are looking for. By the time your book is written, they'll be looking for something else.

Andrew Cowan

I tell writers to keep reading, reading, reading. Read widely and deeply. And I tell them not to give up even after getting rejection letters.

Anita Diamant

I started reading literature at 17 or 18, and I
felt this extra beat to life.

Richard Ford

Sometimes reading other writers helps. You
learn some little technique that turns out to be
useful, or simply are re-inspired by the
amazing things others do.

M. T. Anderson

I wouldn't be a very good writer if someone
hadn't taught me how to read.

Richard Ford

I guess the important thing for young writers
is to read.

Paul Auster

If you want to be a writer, don't worry so
much about writing. Read as much as you can.
Read as many different writers as you can.
Soak up the styles. You can learn all kinds of
ways to say things.

R. L. Stine

Reading is probably what leads most writers
to writing.

Richard Ford

To be a good writer, read a lot and write every day.

Neil Gaiman

To learn to read is to light a fire; every syllable that is spelled out is a spark.

Victor Hugo

When I write a novel I start each morning by reading for 20 minutes.

Richard Ford

Read as much as you possibly can. Nothing will help you as much as reading and you'll go through a phase where you will imitate your favorite writers and that's fine because that's a learning experience, too.

J. K. Rowling

While you're writing, read like mad – but read analytically. You will never be able to put a book together without an understanding of how other books work. I suspect that this is more a matter of instinct than anything else – but you can nurture that instinct by looking at other texts and thinking, "What's successful here? What's failing? And why?"

Sarah Waters

4

The Solitude of Writing

Writing is a product of silence.

Carrie Latet

Solitude.
It is way underrated in our world
of writing, We stay busy. We act busy.
We thrive on busy. The truth is
there is a lot of beauty
that lives in the solitude.
Quiet is not the enemy.
Quiet is necessary
for brains to not self-destruct.

Bonnie Baker

The first thing that distinguishes a writer is that he is most alive when alone.

Martin Amis

In utter loneliness, a writer tries to explain the inexplicable and if he is a writer wise enough to know it can't be done, then he is not a writer at all. A good writer always works at the impossible.

John Steinbeck

It's true that it's a solitary occupation, but you would be surprised at how much companionship a group of imaginary characters can offer once you get to know them.

Anne Tyler

Even though I get a lot done with my solitude, and I make the best use of it possible, I always think solitude is an interlude in a period of time, which is populated by others.

Richard Ford

I need solitude for my writing; not like a hermit—that wouldn't be enough—but like a dead man.

Franz Kafka

When I'm writing solitude feels very good.
But when I'm not writing it feels lonely.

Michael Chabon

I'm afraid my closely guarded solitude causes some hurt feelings now and then. But how to explain, without wounding someone, that you want to be wholly in the world you are writing about, that it would take two days to get the visitor's voice out of the house so that you could listen to your own characters again?

Margaret Bourke-White

I love writing, and I love the solitude of the writing, in that you're just sitting there creating something from nothing, or a new story for characters you love and care about.

John Wells

The place of stillness that you have to go to write, but also to read seriously, is the point where you can actually make responsible decisions, where you can actually engage productively with an otherwise scary and unmanageable world.

Jonathan Frazen

The monotony and solitude of a quiet life stimulates the creative mind.

Albert Einstein

The only environment the artist needs is whatever peace, whatever solitude, and whatever pleasure he can get at not too high a cost.

William Faulkner

Writing is something you do alone. It's a profession for introverts who want to tell you a story but don't want to make eye contact while doing it.

John Green

Writing is utter solitude, the descent into the cold abyss of oneself.

Franz Kafka

Without great solitude, no serious work is possible.

Picasso

Writing is a lonely job; you have to read, and then you must sit down at the desk and write. There's no one there to tell you when to write, what to write, or how to write. I tell students if they are going to be writers, they must sit down at a desk and write every day.

Ernest J. Gaines

In utter loneliness a writer tries to explain the inexplicable and if he is a writer wise enough to know it can't be done, then he is not a writer at all. A good writer always works at the impossible.

John Steinbeck

Writers seem to me to be people who need to retire from social life and do a lot of thinking about what's happened—almost to calm themselves.

Helen Garner

Writing is mostly an isolating experience … I think the time in isolation is reflective time, and reflection is good for fiction writing. It may be good for creativity in general.

Rick Moody

As a writer, I need an enormous amount of time alone. Writing is 90 percent procrastination: reading magazines, eating cereal out of the box, watching infomercials. It's a matter of doing everything you can to avoid writing, until it is four in the morning and you reach the point where you have to write. Having anybody watching that or attempting to share it with me would be grisly.

Paul Rudnik

It is undoubtedly a lonely career, but I suspect that people who find it terribly lonely are not writers. I think if you are a writer you realize how valuable the time is when you are absolutely alone with your characters in complete peace.

P. D. James

Writing is a fairly lonely business unless you invite people in to watch you do it, which is often distracting and then you have to ask them to leave.

Marc Lawrence

Writing is the most fun you can have by yourself.

Terry Prachett

Writing is a product of silence.

Carrie Latet

The first thing that distinguishes a writer is that he is most alive when alone.

Martin Amis

Writing is a lonely job. Even if a writer socializes regularly, when he gets down to the real business of his life, it is he and his type writer or word processor. No one else is or can be involved in the matter.

Isaac Asimov

v

5

Get Started!

This is how you do it: you sit down at the keyboard and you put one word after another until it's done. It's that easy, and that hard.

Neil Gaiman

If the first line of your story doesn't grab readers, they'll never read the second. Hook them with the lead and keep the good stuff coming. Even when you're writing non-fiction, writing has to be entertaining for people to stick around. Pay attention to how you finish things. Don't just restate the lead—circle back to an opening anecdote, close with a bang-up quote, or simply finish telling the story.

William Zinsser

If I waited for perfection, I would never write a word.

Margaret Atwood

Writing is not like dancing or modeling; it's not something where—if you missed it by age 19—you're finished. It's never too late. Your writing will only get better as you get older and wiser. If you writing something beautiful and important, and the right person somehow discovers it, they will clear room for you on the bookshelves of the world—at any age. At least try.

Elizabeth Gilbert

Almost all good writing begins with terrible first efforts. You need to start somewhere.

Anne Lamott

If you wait for inspiration to write, you're not a writer, you're a waiter.

Dan Poynter

I always start every book with a question I don't know the answer to. So I think that by writing it, I discover it.

Soman Chainani

On a blank leaf I scrawled: "In a hole in the

ground there lived a rabbit." I did not and do not know why.

J. R. R. Tolkien

Planning to write is not writing. Outlining, researching, talking to people about what you're doing, none of that is writing. Writing is writing.

E. L. Doctorow

Get it down. Take chances. It may bad, but it's the only way you can do anything really good.

William Faulkner

A day will come when the story inside you will want to breathe on its own. That's when you'll start writing.

Sarah Noffke

Bad writing precedes good writing. This is an infallible rule, so don't waste time trying to avoid bad writing. (That just slows down the process.) Anything committed to paper can be changed. The idea is to start, and then go from there.

Janet Hulstrand

You might not write well every day, but you

can always edit a bad page. You can't edit a blank page.

Jodi Picoult

If you want to write, you can. Fear stops most people from writing, not lack of talent, whatever that is. Who am I? What right have I to speak? Who will listen to me if I do? You're a human being, with a unique story to tell, and you have every right. If you speak with passion, many of us will listen. We need stories to live, all of us. We live by story. Yours enlarges the circle.

Richard Rhodes

There are a thousand thoughts lying within a man that he does not know until he takes up the pen to write.

William Makepeace Thackeray

The scariest moment is always just before you start.

Stephen King

Don't start with writing a best-seller. Start with writing a good line. Don't self-publish hoping to get rich. Do it hoping to find ten readers who will become stalwart fans.

M. J. Rose

You can, you should, and if you're brave
enough to start, you will.

Stephen King

The worst enemy to creativity is self-doubt.

Sylvia Plath

Start writing sooner. Don't wait for
permission. Don't hesitate.

Robin Hobb

I hate outlines. I have a broad sense of where
the story is going; I know the end, I know the
end of the principal characters, and I know
the major turning points and events from the
books, the climaxes for each book, but I don't
necessarily know each twist and turn along the
way. That's something I discover in the course
of writing and that's what makes writing
enjoyable. I think if I outlined
comprehensively and stuck to the outline the
actual writing would be boring.

George R. R. Martin

There is no greater agony than bearing an
untold story inside you.

Maya Angelou

Every minute that I waste watching TV or playing on Facebook some other writer is writing my book.

Darlene Schacht

Ask yourself if what you're doing today is getting you closer to where you want to be tomorrow.

Unknown

If you want something you've never had you have to do something you've never done.

Unknown

Stop waiting for Friday, for summer, for someone to fall in love with you, for life. Happiness is achieved when you stop waiting for it and make the most of the moment you are in now.
Unknown

It is never too late to be what you might have been.

George Eliot

Don't call it a dream. Call it a plan.

Unknown

Don't be a 'writer.' Be writing.

William Faulkner

To write something you have to risk making a fool of yourself.

Anne Rice

In order to write the book you want to write, in the end you have to become the person you need to become to write that book.

Junot Diaz

Thinking about writing, and putting pen to paper
is the difference between a dreamer and a writer.

Darlene Schacht

So this is always the key: you have to write the book you love, the book that's alive in your heart. That's the one you have to write.

Lurleen McDaniel

There's a secret that real writers know that wannabe writers don't, and the secret is this: it's not the writing part that's hard. What's hard is sitting down to write.

Steven Pressfield

How vain it is to sit down to write when you have not stood up to live.

Henry David Thoreau

I'm writing a book. I've got the page numbers done.

Steven Wright

Writing is an exploration. You start from nothing and learn as you go.

E. L. Doctorow

We see the brightness of a new page where everything yet can happen.

Rainer Maria Rilke

Thousands of people plan to be writers, but they never get around to it. The only way to find out if you can write is to set aside a certain period every day and try.

Judith Krantz

There is something delicious about writing the first word of a story. You never quite know where they'll take you.

Beatrix Potter

Writing the opening lines of a story is a bit like starting to ski at the steepest part of a hill.

You must have all your skills under control from the first instant.

Marion Dane Bauer

If you want to be a writer stop talking about it and sit down and write!

Jackie Collins

The first sentence of a book is a handshake, perhaps an embrace. Style and personality are irrelevant. They can be formal or casual. They can be tall or short or fat or thin. They can obey the rules or break them. But they need to contain a charge, a live current, which shocks and illuminates.

Jhumpa Lahir

Starting a novel is opening a door on a misty landscape; you can still see very little but you can smell the earth and feel the wind blowing.

Iris Murdoch

An opening line should invite the reader to begin the story. It should say: Listen. Come in here. You want to know about this.

Stephen King

Getting started on writing a book isn't as hard as it sounds. You don't need a plan and an outline. In fact, all you need are two things: time and one idea.

Natasha Lester

The scariest moment is always just before you start.

Stephen King

Sometimes the hardest thing in writing a story is where to start. You don't need to have a great idea, you just have to put pen to paper. Start with a bad idea, start with the wrong direction, start with a character you don't like. Something positive will come out of it.

Marion Deuchars

It's the job that's never started takes longest to finish.

J. R. R. Tolkien

There is no excuse. If you want to write, write. This is your life; you are responsible for it. You will not live forever. Don't wait. Make the time now.

Natalie Goldberg

A writer who waits for ideal conditions under

which to work will die without putting a word
on paper.

E. B. White

Inspiration is for amateurs—the rest of us just
show up and get to work.

Chuck Close

Writers write while dreamers procrastinate.

Besa Kosova

Whatever is not started will never get finished.

Johann Wolfgang von Goethe

Finish your novel, because you learn more
that way than any other.

James Scott Bell

Start writing, no matter what. The water does
not flow until the faucet is turned on.

Louis L'Amour

The pages are still blank, but there is a
miraculous feeling of the words being there,
written in invisible ink and clamoring to
become visible.

Vladimir Nabokov

The blank page is yours. Cast aside worries over art and criticism. Imagine a land without rules.

Chuck Wendig

When you have no choice, when it haunts you, that's the time you tell your story.

Edwidge Danticat

Remember that nothing would get done at all if a person waited until he could do it so well that no one could find fault with it.

Sheila Waters

There comes a point in your life when you need to stop reading other people's books and write your own.

Albert Einstein

If you're going to be a writer, the first essential is to just write. Do not wait for an idea. Start writing something and the ideas will come.

Louis L'Amour

Don't just plan to write—write. It is only by writing, not dreaming about it, that we develop our own style.

P. D. James

Write while the heat is in you. The writer who postpones the recording of his thoughts uses an iron which has cooled to burn a hole with. He cannot inflame the minds of his audience.

Henry David Thoreau

The act of writing stimulates thought, so when you cannot think of anything to write, start writing anyway.

Barbara Fine Clouse

If I waited till I felt like writing, I'd never write at all.

Anne Tyler

6
Staying With It

First, forget inspiration.
Habit is more dependable.
Habit will sustain you whether you're
inspired or not. Habit will help you
finish and polish your stories.
Inspiration won't. Habit is persistence
in practice.

Octavia Butler

When I type a title page,
I hold it and I look at it and I think,
I just need four thousand sentences
to go with this and I'll have a book!

Betsy Byars

Write until you surprise yourself.

Frances Caballo

Abandon the idea that you are ever going to
finish. Lose track of the 400 pages and write
just one page for each day. It helps. Then
when it gets finished,
you are always surprised.

John Steinbeck

The way to write a book is to actually write a
book. A pen is useful, typing is also good.
Keep putting words on the page.

Anne Enright

Just finish. Even if it's horrible—most of my
first drafts are terrible—but finish it anyways.

Amy Tintera

You only fail if you stop writing.

Ray Bradbury

Persistence counts for a lot. I wrote my first
book from 4 to 6 a.m. over three years,
starting when my daughter was 4 months old.
I just never gave up. People say there is not
enough time, but there is. If I can do it,

anyone can do it.

Nicola Yoon

Finish your novel, because you learn more
that way
than any other.

James Scott Bell

It is worth mentioning, for future reference,
that the creative power which bubbles so
pleasantly in beginning a new book quiets
down after a time, and one goes on more
steadily. Doubts creep in. Then one becomes
resigned. Determination not to give in, and
the sense of an impending shape keep one at
it more than anything.

Virginia Woolf

When I face the desolate impossibility of
writing 500 pages, a sick sense of failure falls
on me, and I know I can never do it. Then
gradually, I write one page and then another.
One day's work is all I can permit myself to
complete.

John Steinbeck

Remember, people may keep you (or me)
from being a published author but no one can
stop you from being a writer. All you have to

do is write. And keep writing. While you're working at a career, while you're raising children, while you're trout fishing—keep writing! No one can stop you but you.

Katherine Neville

In my view a writer is a writer because even when there is no hope, even when nothing you do shows any sign of promise, you keep writing anyway.

Junot Diaz

The process of writing a novel is like taking a journey by boat. You have to continually set yourself on course. If you get distracted or allow yourself to drift, you will never make it to the destination.

Walter Mosley

Successful writers are not the ones who write the best sentences. They are the ones who keep writing. They are the ones who discover what is most important and strangest and most pleasurable in themselves, and keep believing in the value of their work, despite the difficulties.

Bonnie Friedman

Exercise the writing muscle every day, even if it is only a letter, notes, a title list, a character sketch, a journal entry. Writers are like dancers, like athletes. Without that exercise, the muscles seize up.

Jane Yolen

Don't be paralyzed by the idea that you are writing a book; just write.

Isabelle Allende

With writing … you must keep in the habit. After a lapse it will take you not an hour, but a week, a month, maybe, to find your mood again—that mood in which things drop from heaven.

Anne Bosworth Greene

Write every day, line by line, page by page, hour by hour. Do this despite fear. For above all else, beyond imagination and skill, what the world asks of you is courage, courage to risk rejection, ridicule and failure.

Robert McKee

If you want to be a writer, you have to write every day … you don't go to a well once but daily.

Walter Mosley

Write a lot. And I mean a lot. I once read that

being a writer was not a hobby, it was an affliction … If you really are one of the afflicted then this piece of advice won't apply since nothing can stop you from continuing. If you aren't afflicted then perhaps you really should consider some better use of your time.

Simon Scarrow

When you sit down to write, write. Don't do anything else except go to the bathroom, and only do that if it absolutely cannot be put off.

Stephen King

Write your heart out and persevere, persevere, persevere!

Ellen Banda-Aaku

A writer never finds the time to write. A writer makes it. If you don't have the drive, the discipline, and the desire, then you can have all the talent in the world, and you aren't going to finish a book.

Nora Roberts

The thing all writers do best is find ways to avoid writing

Alan Dean Foster

Write while the heat is in you. The writer who

postpones the recording of his thoughts uses an iron which has cooled to burn a hole with. He cannot inflame the minds of his audience.

Henry David Thoreau

Once writing has become your major vice and greatest pleasure only death can stop it.

Ernest Hemingway

Serious writers write, inspired or not. Over time they discover that routine is a better friend than inspiration.

Ralph Keyes

I made a startling discovery. Time spent writing=output of work. Amazing.

Ann Patchett

Work. Write. Read. Write some more. Read some more. Keep putting words on the page or screen, because that's the only way you'll get better.

S. J. Watson

Don't give up. You'll have setbacks and sometimes it'll seem like it's never going to happen. But don't stop. I'll say it again, don't ever stop.

Patrick Ness

A word after a word after a word is power.

Margaret Atwood

A professional writer is an amateur who didn't quit.

Richard Bach

Best advice on writing I've ever received. Finish.

Peter Mayle

When you finish a draft of a poem, or short story or novel, you make sure you go out and celebrate all night long because whether the world ever notices or not, whether you get it published or not, you did something most people never do: You started, stuck with, and finished a creative work. And that is a triumph.

Andre Dubus III

It is doubtful that anyone with an internet connection at his workplace is writing good fiction.

Jonathon Franzen

Here is the cruel irony of the blank page: While it lures us with its pristine landscape, we must first cover it with mud. There is simply no other way to write. It is a brutal act of faith. In writing, we must unleash a mess onto the page and then reach inward and grab hold of every last thread of trust, believing without sight that: "It will be beautiful. You'll see. Just don't walk away."

Christin Taylor

Advice to young writers who want to get ahead without annoying delays: Don't write about man, write about a man.

E. B. White

Put your heart and soul on the page.

Victoria Zachheim

A writer is working when he is staring out the window.

Burton Rascoe

Writers see the world differently. Every voice we hear, every face we see, every hand we touch could become story fabric.

Buffy Andrews

Imagine what you are writing about. See it and live it. Do not think it up laboriously, as if you were working out mental arithmetic. Just look at it, touch it, smell it, listen to it, turn yourself into it. When you do this, the words look after themselves, like magic.

Ted Hughes

I just write what I wanted to write. I write what amuses me. It's totally for myself.

J. K. Rowling

I didn't set out to write this book. It crept up on me when I wasn't looking, when I didn't know I was writing it.

Mark David Gerson

Honing your ability to observe accurately—and to write down what you've noticed—must be part of your lifelong commitment to fiction.

Jack M. Bickham

If you're going to be a writer, he first essential is just to write. Do not wait for an idea. Start writing something and the ideas will come.

Louis L'Amour

Many times I just sit for three hours with no ideas coming to me. But I know one thing: if an idea does come between nine and twelve, I am there ready for it.

Flannery O'Connor

You must stay drunk on writing so reality cannot destroy you.

Ray Bradbury

The best time for planning a book is while you're doing the dishes.

Agatha Christie

I think I did pretty well, considering I started out with nothing but a bunch of blank paper.
Steve Martin

A writer lives, at best, in a state of astonishment. Beneath any feeling he has of the good or evil of the world lies a deeper one of wonder at it all.

William Sansom

Creativity is piercing the mundane to find the marvelous.

Bill Moyers

The discipline of the writer is to learn to be still and listen to what his subject has to tell him.

Rachel Carson

You must write it all out, at any cost. Writing

is thinking. It is more than living, for it is being conscious of living.

Anne Morrow Lindbergh

The deeper you can listen, the better you can write.

Natalie Goldberg

Write what disturbs you, what you fear, what you have not been willing to speak about. Be willing to be split open.

Natalie Goldberg

What people are ashamed of usually makes a good story.

F. Scott Fitzgerald

To write, you need to find what you love.

D. J. McHale

Novels begin, not on the page, but in meditation and day-dreaming—in thinking, not writing.

Joyce Carol Oates

But with writers, there's nothing wrong with melancholy. It's an important color in writing.

Paul McCartney

If I started to wait for moments of inspiration, I would never finish a book. Inspiration for me comes from a regular effort.

Mario Vargas Llosa

Whether you want to entertain or to provoke, to break hearts or reassure them, what you bring to your writing must consist of your longings and disappointments.

Rafael Yglesias

The secret of it all, is to write in the gush, the throb, the flood, of the moment—to put things down without deliberation—without worrying about their style—without waiting for a fit time or place. I always worked that way. I took the first scrap of paper, the first doorstep, the first desk, and wrote—wrote, wrote … By writing at the instant the very heartbeat of life is caught.

Walt Whitman

Have more than one idea on the go at any one time. If it's a choice between writing a book and doing nothing I will always choose the latter. It's only if I have an idea for two books that I choose one rather than the other. I always have to feel that I'm bunking off from something.

Geoff Dyer

And by the way, everything in life is writable about if you have the outgoing guts to do it, and the imagination to improvise. The worst enemy to creativity is self-doubt.

Sylvia Plath

A writer's job is to imagine everything so personally that the fiction is as vivid as memories.

John Irving

Ideas aren't magical; the only tricky part is holding on to one long enough to get it written down.

Lynn Abbey

Live your life as a curious person. Try to see the entire world as your muse. Ask questions. Dismiss nothing. Eavesdrop. Always eavesdrop. You'll have more fun, learn all the time, and when the time comes to sit down and write, you'll have a whole line-up of stories just waiting to be told.

Lauren Kate

Following that scavenger hunt of curiosity can lead you to amazing, unexpected places.

Elizabeth Gilbert

At night, when the objective world has slunk back into its cavern and left dreamers to their own, there come inspirations and capabilities impossible at any less magical and quiet hour. No one knows whether or not he is a writer unless he has tried writing at night.

H.P. Lovecraft

First forget inspiration. Habit is more dependable. Habit will sustain you whether you're inspired or not. Habit will help you finish and polish your stories. Inspiration won't. Habit is persistence in practice.

Octavia E. Butler

Words - so innocent and powerless as they are, as standing in a dictionary, how potent for good and evil they become in the hands of one who knows how to combine them.

Nathaniel Hawthorne

Anybody who has survived his childhood has enough information about life to last him the rest of his days.

Flannery O'Connor

Throw up into your typewriter every morning.
Clean up every noon.

Raymond Chandler

Inspiration comes of working every day.

Charles Baudelaire

The creations of a great writer are little more
than the moods and passions of his own
heart, given surnames and Christian names,
and sent to walk the earth.

William Butler Yeats

Writing is a job, a talent, but it's also the place
to go in your head. It is the imaginary friend
you drink your tea with in the afternoon.

Ann Patchett

Write down everything that comes to you in
an adrenalin rush in the small hours, and on
waking up. About one-half—truly—will turn
out to be useful and it sets you up for the
morning work.

Laura Cumming

A writer lives, at best, in a state of
astonishment. Beneath any feeling he has of

the good or evil of the world lies a deeper one
of wonder at it all.

William Sansom

Don't loaf and invite inspiration; light out
after it with a club, and if you don't get it you
will nonetheless get something that looks
remarkably like it.

Jack London

You never have to change anything you got
up in the middle of the night to write.

Saul Bellow

All you need to do is write one word after
another. Don't think about the whole novel,
or about what you've written, just think about
the next word.

Karen Woodward

Yet, one mistake we make is we don't tackle
the novel when we're tired. We believe our
work will be better if we've rested. This isn't
necessarily true.

Kristen Lamb

What amazes me is that most days feel
useless. I don't seem to accomplish
anything—just a few pages, most of which

don't seem very good. Yet, when I put all those wasted days together, I somehow end up with a book of which I'm very proud.

Louis Sachar

I've been writing since I was six. It is a compulsion, so I can't really say where the desire came from; I've always had it. My breakthrough with the first book came through persistence, because a lot of publishers turned it down!

J. K. Rowling

You have to simply love writing, and you have to remind yourself often that you love it.

Susan Orlean

Don't be paralyzed by the idea that you're writing a book; just write.

Isabelle Allende

You'll never change your life until you change something you do daily. The secret of your success is found in your daily routine.

John C. Maxwell

What you do every day matters more than what you do once in a while.

Gretchen Rubin

An arrow can only be shot by pulling it backward. So when life is dragging you back with difficulties, it means that it's going to launch you into something great. So just focus, and keep aiming.

Unknown

If you can't stop thinking about it, don't stop working for it.

Unknown

If you want to be a writer, you have to write every day … You don't skip a child's breakfast or forget to wake up in the morning.

Walter Mosley

Make sure your family and loved ones don't interrupt you during your writing time. If you're a lawyer or doctor, friends don't just stop by the office to chat or interrupt you from your work. But for some reason, people think writing is different. It isn't, and you need to make clear that this is sacred time.

Douglas Preston

I decided that I would continue to write as long as I lived, even if I never sold one thing, because that was what I wanted out of my life.

George Bernau

Even the most productive writers are expert dawdlers.

Donald M. Murray

Practice—write every day even if it's only for ten minutes. Remember, nothing is wasted. Eventually your style will emerge. Persevere!

Eoin Colfer

The people who succeed in the arts most often are the people who get up and again after getting knocked down. Persistence is critical.

Scott Turow

I do not so much write a book as sit up with it, as a dying friend. I hold its hand and hope it will get better.

Annie Dillard

Inspiration is wonderful when it happens but the writer must develop an approach for the rest of the time. The wait is simply too long.

Leonard Bernstein

Write every day, just to keep in the habit, and remember that whatever you have written is neither as good nor as bad as you think it is.

Just keep going, and tell yourself that you will fix it later.

Jane Smiley

Keep scribbling! Something will happen.

Frank McCourt

There comes a time in your life when you have to choose to turn the page, write another book or simply close it.

Shannon L. Alder

You must keep sending work out; you must never let a manuscript do nothing but eat its head off in a drawer. You send that work out again and again, while you're working on another one. If you have talent, you will receive some measure of success—but only if you persist.

Isaac Asimov

Try looking at your mind as a wayward puppy that you are trying to paper train. You don't drop-kick a puppy into the neighbor's yard every time it piddles on the floor. You just keep bringing it back to the newspaper.

Anne Lamott

Write every day, line by line, page by page,

hour by hour. Do this despite fear. For above all else, beyond imagination and skill, what the world asks of you is courage, courage to risk rejection, ridicule and failure. As you follow the quest for stories told with meaning and beauty, study thoughtfully but write boldly. Then, like the hero of the fable, your dance will dazzle the world.

Robert McKee

The first thing you have to know about writing is that it is something you must do every day. There are two reasons for this rule: Getting the work done
and connecting with your unconscious mind.
Walter Mosley

My most important discovery is that I have optimum hours for writing. These are between 10:00 am and 2:00 pm. For a lifetime I've told myself that I was a night-time writer—it seemed romantic. But actually I'm tired at night, and that's when I prefer to read and research. Whatever your optimum hours are, don't cheat yourself of them.

Amy Wallace

First, if you want to write, you need to keep

an honest, unpublishable journal that nobody reads, nobody but you. Where you just put down what you think about life, what you think about things, what you think is fair and what you think is unfair. And second, you need to read. You can't be a writer if you're not a reader. It's the great writers who teach us how to write. The third thing is to write. Just write a little bit every day. Even if it's for only half an hour—write, write, write.

Madeleine L'Engle

The secret of becoming a writer is to write, write and keep on writing.

Ken MacLeod

Successful writers are not the ones who write the best sentences. They are the ones who keep writing. They are the ones who discover what is most important and strangest and most pleasurable in themselves, and keep believing in the value of their work, despite the difficulties.

Bonnie Friedman

Don't quit. It's very easy to quit during the first ten years. Nobody cares whether you write or not, and it's very hard to write when nobody cares one way or the other. You can't get fired if you don't write, and most of the time you don't get rewarded if you do. But don't quit.

Andre Dubus II

Work. Write. Read. Write some more. Read some more. Keep putting words on the page or screen, because that's the only way you'll get better.

S. J. Watson

Writing may or may not be your salvation; it might or might not be your destiny. But that does not matter. What matters right now are the words, one after another. Find the next word. Write it down.

Neil Gaiman

Sit down and write. Just sit down and write. Everything else can wait.

Joanna Rakoff

A word after a word after a word is power.

Margaret Atwood

I believe that anything is possible if you have the combination of love for what you're doing and the will to sit down and not get up until it's done.

Kaye Gibbons

The first thing you have to know about writing is that it is something you must do every day. There are two reasons for this rule: Getting the work done and connecting with your unconscious mind.

Walter Mosley

I, even now, persist in believing that these black marks on white paper bear the greatest significance, that if I keep writing I might be able to catch the rainbow of consciousness in a jar.

Jeffrey Eugenides

I'm a huge fan of Stephen King's "bum glue" idea: attaching yourself to a chair (or wherever you write, or have ideas) and just working very, very hard.

Brooke Davis

Work every day. No matter what has happened the day or night before, get up and bite on the nail.

Ernest Hemingway

Finish everything you start.

Colm Toibin

Write. The only thing that matters is getting words on paper. It doesn't matter if you write the book in a straight line, if you use an outline, if you write it in little pieces and glue them together. Even backward. Writing is the only way you'll discover what works for you.

Diana Gabaldon

Finish. The difference between being a writer and being a person of talent is the discipline it takes to apply the seat of your pants to the seat of your chair and finish. Don't talk about doing it. Do it. Finish.

E. L. Konigsburg

It isn't self-belief that gets me to the end of a book; it's the sheer bloody-mindedness to keep writing anyway, no matter the prospects, or the possibility of it being rubbish.

Natasha Lester

If you don't write when you don't have time for it, you won't write when you do have time for it.

Katerina Stoykova Klemer

Set a goal each week for your writing and work to reach it. Wake up every morning and treat it like a job. It's all about regularity. Read back what you've written and ask yourself, "Do I enjoy this? Does it work?" If you're stumbling over something as you read it, rewrite, rewrite, rewrite!

Sharon Grenham-Thompson

When I'm writing, I write. And then it's as if the muse is convinced that I'm serious and says, 'Okay. Okay. I'll come.'

Maya Angelou

Be ruthless about protecting writing days. Do not cave into endless requests to have "essential" and "long overdue" meetings on those days.

J. K. Rowling

Being a good writer is 3% talent, 97% not being distracted by the Internet.

Unknown

Write 1,000 words a day, five days a week, before you do anything else. If you do it first thing in the morning, then you won't get distracted by all the things that tempt you not to write.

Lisa See

A day of bad writing is always better than a day of no writing.

Don Roff

Don't listen to people who tell you that very few people get published and you won't be one of them. Don't listen to your friend who says you are better than Tolkien and don't have to try any more. Keep writing, keep faith in the idea that you have unique stories to tell, and tell them. I meet far too many people who are going to be writers "someday." When they are out of high school, when they've finished college, after the wedding, when the kids are older, after I retire … That is such a trap. You will never have any more free time than you do right now. So, whether you are 12 or 70, you should sit down today and start being a writer if that is what you want to do. You might have to write on a notebook while your kids are playing on the swings or write in your car on your coffee break. That's okay. I think we've all "been there, done that." It all starts with the writing.

Robin Hobb

You don't need endless time and perfect conditions. Do it now. Do it today. Do it for twenty minutes and watch your heart start beating.

Barbara Sher

As cows need milking and sweet peas need picking, so writers must continually exercise their mental muscles by a daily stint.

Joan Aiken

Remember, people may keep you (or me) from being a published author but no one can stop you from being a writer. All you have to do is write. And keep writing. While you're working at a career, while you're raising children, while you're trout fishing—keep writing! No one can stop you but you.

Katherine Nerville

The people who succeed in the arts most often are the people who get up again after getting knocked down. Persistence is critical.

Scott Turow

You must learn to hush the demons that whisper, "No one wants to read this. This has already been said. Your voice doesn't matter."

In the rare moments when the voices finally hush, you might hear the angels sing.

Margaret Feinberg

A writer is a writer not because she writes well and easily, because she has amazing talent, or because everything she does is golden. A writer is a writer because, even when there is no hope, even when nothing you do shows any sign of promise, you keep writing anyway.

Junot Diaz

You have to write when you're not inspired. And you have to write the scenes that don't inspire you. And the weird thing is that six months later, a year later, you'll look back at them and you can't remember which scenes you wrote when you were inspired and which scenes you just wrote because they had to be written next.

Neil Gaiman

Stop in the middle of a sentence, leaving a rough edge for you to start from the next day—that way, you can write three or five words without being "creative" and before you know it, you're writing.

Cory Doctorow

Serious writers write, inspired or not. Over time they discover that routine is a better friend than inspiration.

Ralph Keyes

Write a short story every week. It's not possible to write 52 bad short stories in a row.

Ray Bradbury

One thing that helps is to give myself permission to write badly. I tell myself that I'm going to do my five or 10 pages no matter what, and that I can always tear them up the following morning if I want. I'll have lost nothing—writing and tearing up five pages would leave me no further behind than if I took the day off.

Lawrence Block

The only way to learn to write is to force yourself to produce a certain amount of words on a regular basis.

William Zinsser

Be ruthless about protecting writing days, i.e., do not cave in to endless requests to have "essential" and "long overdue" meetings on those days.

J. K. Rowling

nobody has time to write a book. Some
people just do it anyhow.

Sharyn McCrumb

The difference between writers who finish
books and those who don't—is that the
finishers don't stop writing until they get to:
THE END.

Bryan Hutchinson

7

The Hard Work of Writing

There is nothing to writing.
All you do is sit down
at a typewriter and bleed.

Ernest Hemingway

The only people who think writing
is easy are people who don't write.
Writing's a difficult, courageous act.
Bravery is required,
as well as a great deal
of slogging along.
A lot of our work is work.

Gillian Roberts

This morning I took out a comma and this afternoon I put it back again.

Oscar Wilde

Be prepared to work harder than ever before, because writing well takes great effort—the better the writing, the greater the effort. Expect a lot of rejections. And don't expect to make a living as a writer, at least not right away.

Patricia O'Conner

If any scene you're writing feels bland and boring, go back and make sure you've used all five senses.

Jean Marie Stine

Write hard and clear about what hurts.

Ernest Hemingway

Writing is a combination of intangible creative fantasy and appallingly hard work.

Anthony Powell

Serious writers write, inspired or not. Over time they discover that routine is a better friend than inspiration.

Ralph Keyes

You know what I did after I wrote my first novel? I shut up and wrote twenty-three more.

Michael Connelly

Write from the soul. The market is fickle; the soul is eternal.

J. Carver

I begin to write. If nothing occurs to me, I remain seated at the writing table until something finally does come to mind. You must surrender yourself to a discipline.

Camilo Jose Cela

Writing is wretched, discouraging, physically unhealthy, infinitely frustrating work. And when it all comes down together it's utterly glorious.

Ralph Peters

There was a moment when I changed from an amateur to a professional. I assumed the burden of a profession, which is to write even when you don't want to, don't much like what you're writing, and aren't writing particularly well.

Agatha Christie

By the time I am nearing the end of a story, the first part will have been reread and altered and corrected at least one hundred and fifty times. I am suspicious of both facility and speed. Good writing is essentially rewriting. I am positive of this.

Roald Dahl

I don't wait for moods. You accomplish nothing if you do that. Your mind must know it has got to get down to work.

Pearl S. Buck

Writing a novel is not merely going on a shopping expedition across the border to an unreal land: it is hours and years spent in the factories, the streets, the cathedrals of the imagination.

Janet Frame

I don't like to write, but I love to have written.

Michael Kanin

We are all apprentices in a craft where no one ever becomes a master.

Ernest Hemingway

Learning to write sound, interesting,

sometimes elegant prose is the work of a lifetime.

Joseph Epstein

A word is not the same with one writer as with another. One tears it from his guts. The other pulls it out of his overcoat pocket.

Charles Peguy

When I sit down to write, which is the essential moment in my life, I am completely alone. Whenever I write a book, I accumulate a lot of documentation. That background material is the most intimate part of my private life. It's a little embarrassing—like being seen in your underwear. It's like the way magicians never tell others how they make a dove come out of a hat.

Gabriel Garcia Marquez

Every writer I know has trouble writing.

Joseph Heller

There is no rule on how to write. Sometimes it comes easily and perfectly; sometimes it is like drilling rock and then blasting it out with charges.

Ernest Hemingway

Writing is thinking. To write well is to think clearly. That's why it's so hard.

David McCullough

If you really want to write, then shut yourself in a room, close the door, and WRITE. If you don't want to write, do something else. It's as simple as that.

Mary Garden

Writing is creative but the guts of it boils down to discipline.

Susan Duncan

The secret of it all is to write … without waiting for a fit time or place.

Walt Whitman

I'm sitting in my office trying to squeeze a story from my head. It is that kind of morning when you feel like melting the typewriter into a bar of steel and clubbing yourself to death with it.

Richard Matheson

Writing is work. It's also gambling. You don't get a pension plan. Other people can help you

a bit, but essentially you're on your own.
Nobody is making you do this: you chose it,
so don't whine.

Margaret Atwood

Writing is hard for normal people. It's not
physically demanding, of course, but writing
requires a mental and emotional exertion that
few people find pleasant.

Brian Wasko

Writing a book is a horrible, exhausting
struggle, like a long bout with some painful
illness. One would never undertake such a
thing if one were not driven on by some
demon whom one can neither resist nor
understand.

George Orwell

No tears in the writer, no tears in the reader.
No surprise for the writer, no surprise for the
reader.

Robert Frost

At its best, the sensation of writing is that of
any unmerited grace. It is handed to you, but
only if you look for it. You search, you break
your heart, your back, your brain, and then—

and only then—it is handed to you.

Annie Dillard

Writers spend three years rearranging 26 letters of the alphabet. It's enough to make you lose your mind day by day.

Richard Price

When fear creeps up your spine, start writing. Shake it off, word by word, and look at the splinters of fear on the floor, shining like broken glass.

Unknown

If you want to be a writer, write. Write and write and write. If you stop, start again. Save everything that you write. If you feel blocked, write through it until you feel your creative juices flowing again. Write. Writing is what makes a writer, nothing more and nothing less.

Anne Rice

When I write, I feel like an armless, legless man with a crayon in his mouth.

Kurt Vonnegut

Every writer I know has trouble writing.
Joseph Heller

Writing a book is an adventure. To begin with it is a toy and an amusement. Then it becomes a mistress, then it becomes a master, then it becomes a tyrant. The last phase is that just as you are about to be reconciled to your servitude, you kill the monster and fling him to the public.
Winston S. Churchill

I am irritated by my own writing. I am like a violinist whose ear is true, but whose fingers refuse to reproduce precisely the sound he hears within.
Gustave Flaubert

If you are in difficulties with a book, try the element of surprise: attack it at an hour when it isn't expecting it.
H.G. Wells

Writing is hard. That's why so few people stick to it and actually finish things. And why you have a right to be immensely proud when you finish something.
Andy Ihnatko

The easiest thing to do on earth is not write.
William Goldman

You build a novel the same way you build a pyramid. One word, one stone at a time, underneath a full moon when the fingers bleed.

Kate Braverman

You can only learn to be a better writer by actually writing. I don't know much about creative writing programs. But they're not telling the truth if they don't teach, one, that writing is hard work and, two, that you have to give up a great deal of life, your personal life, to be a writer.

Doris Lessing

I find that most people know what a story is until they sit down to write one.
Flannery O'Connor

That is the mystery about writing: it comes out of afflictions, out of the gouged times, when the heart is cut open.

Edna O'Brien

We all often feel like we are pulling teeth,

even those writers whose prose ends up being
the most natural and fluid.

Anne Lamott

I still encourage anyone who feels at all
compelled to write to do so. I just try to warn
people who hope to get published that
publication is not all it is cracked up to be.
But writing is.

Anne Lamott

Most authors liken the struggle of writing to
something mighty and macho, like wrestling a
bear. Writing a book is nothing like that. It is
a small, slow crawl to the finish line.

Amy Poehler

Ah yes, the head is full of books. The hard
part is to force them down through the
bloodstream and out through the fingers.

Edward Abbey

The only way you can write the truth is to
assume that what you set down will never be
read. Not by any other person, and not even
by yourself at some later date. Otherwise you
begin excusing yourself. You must see the
writing as emerging like a long scroll of ink
from the index finger of your right hand; you

must see your left hand erasing it.

Margaret Atwood

Writing is hard. That's why so few people stick to it and actually finish things. And why you have a right to be immensely proud when you finish something.

Andy Ihnatko

Write hard and clear about what hurts.

Ernest Hemingway

Writing never came naturally and I still have to force my hand to do it.

Richard Ford

I'm a full-time believer in writing habits … You may be able to do without them if you have genius but most of us only have talent and this is simply something that has to be assisted all the time by physical and mental habits or it dries up and blows away.

Flannery O'Connor

Writing is like driving a car at night. You can see only as far as your headlights, but you can make the whole trip that way.

E. L. Doctorow

Work on a good piece of writing proceeds on three levels: a musical one, where it is composed; an architectural one, where it is constructed; and finally, a textile one, where it is woven.

Walter Benjamin

A writer is never just looking out of a window or staring into space. They are building a universe to share with the world.

Brenda Ashworth Barry

Establish writing habits, whatever they are, a particular time to write, a number of pages that have to be written, a time goal. If you choose my method,
the time goal, write it down as you go. Don't let it be vague.

Gail Carson Levine

The purpose of literature is to turn blood into ink.

T. S. Elliot

A book is so much a part of oneself that in delivering it to the public one feels as if one were pushing one's own child out into the traffic.

Quentin Bell

The thing all writers do best is find ways to avoid writing.

Alan Dean Foster

When we read, we start at the beginning and continue until we reach the end. When we write, we start in the middle and fight our way out.

Vickie Karp

Writing a novel is a terrible experience, during which the hair often falls out and the teeth decay. I'm always irritated by people who imply that writing fiction is an escape from reality. It is a plunge into reality and it's very shocking to the system.

Flannery O'Connor

Writing is like working in a coal mine. You descend into the darkness of your personal soul, prepared to open a vein upon the page, to mine the darkness of your greatest fears.

Thaddeus Howze

A writer never has a vacation. for a writer life consists of either writing or thinking about writing.

Eugene Ionesco

There is really no prescription for creative work. I heard a writer say the other day that he sits down at the keyboard and the first thing he says to himself is "I don't know."

Geoff Talbot

People on the outside think there's something magical about writing, that you go up in the attic at midnight and cast the bones and come down in the morning with a story, but it isn't like that. You sit in back of the typewriter and you work, and that's all there is to it.

Harlan Ellison

It comes down to hours and hours of work. I rewrite every novel no fewer than four times, sometimes as many as nine times. You can't believe how many hours that consumes.

Ridley Pearson

Writing a first novel takes so much effort, with such little promise of result or reward, that it must necessarily be a labor of love bordering on madness.

Steven Saylor

Writing requires, more than anything else, tremendous discipline. At the end of the day, whilst there are times when it is wonderfully creative and fun, a lot of the time it is just a job. And that means showing up whether you feel like it or not. It also means you write, whether you are inspired or not, and the only way to unlock your creativity is to start writing.

Jane Green

A writer is working when he's staring out the window.

Burton Rascoe

Forget discovery. Think about discipline. Writing is a habit—a physical habit. You can't wait for the muse—you must just sit down at the same time every day and do your work.

Ayelet Waldman

Writing is hard work. A clear sentence is no accident. Very few sentences come out right the first time, or even the third time. Remember this in moments of despair. If you find that writing is hard, it's because it is hard.

William Zinsser

When you can't create, you can work.

Henry Miller

You must want to enough. Enough to take all

the rejections, enough to pay the price of disappointment and discouragement while you are learning. Like any other artist, you are learning your craft—then you can add all the genius you like.

Phyllis Whitney

Amateurs sit and wait for inspiration; the rest of us just get up and go to work.

Stephen King

8

Making Your Writing Sharper

Writing has laws of perspective, of light and shade just as painting does, or music. If you are born knowing them, fine. If not, learn them. Then rearrange the rules to suit yourself.

Truman Capote

Three words for a writer:
Make me care.

Buffy Andrews

In writing, your audience is one single reader.
I have found that sometimes it helps to pick
out one person—a real person you know, or
an imagined person and write to that one.

John Steinbeck

I want the reader to turn the page and keep
on turning to the end. This is accomplished
only when the narrative moves steadily ahead,
not when it comes to a standstill, overloaded
with every item uncovered in the research.

Barbara Tuchman

If there's one thing that divides the amateur
from the professional fiction writer, it's the
tautness of their prose style. Amateur writers'
sentences often meander, twist and turn; they
use many more words than required; and
over-complicate their syntax in an effort to
sound sophisticated. This can end up
confusing readers, as well as slowing down the
action of their story. An agent or
commissioning editor will reject a manuscript
with writing like this before they reach the
bottom of the page.

Rethink Press

The road to hell is paved with adverbs.

Stephen King

As to the adjective, when in doubt, strike it out.

Mark Twain

A story really isn't any good unless it successfully resists paraphrase, unless it hangs on and expands in the mind.

Flannery O'Connor

Never use a long word where a short one will do.

George Orwell

That you can learn to write better is one of our fundamental assumptions. No sensible person would deny the mystery of talent, or for that matter the mystery of inspiration. But if it is vain to deny these mysteries, it is useless to depend on them. No other art form is so infinitely mutable. Writing is revision. All prose responds to work.

Tracy Kidder

You cannot hope to sweep someone else away

by the force of your writing until it has been
done to you.

Stephen King

You don't see the prose, you see the story.
The prose is a window, beyond which all
these wonderful things are happening. If you
start fiddling with tense, people pay attention
to the window instead of what's happening
beyond it.

Brandon Sanderson

It's nouns and verbs, not their assistants, that
give good writing its toughness and color.

William Strunk, Jr.

Don't use words too big for the subject.
Don't say "infinitely" when you mean "very";
otherwise you'll have no word left when you
want to talk about something really infinite.

C. S. Lewis

Good writing is supposed to evoke sensation
in the reader—not the fact that it is raining,
but the feeling of being rained upon.

E. L. Doctorow

However great a man's natural talent may be,

the act of writing cannot be learned all at once.

Jean Jacques Rousseau

The main rule of writing is that if you do it with enough assurance and confidence, you're allowed to do whatever you like. So write your story as it needs to be written. Write it honestly, and tell it as best you can. I'm not sure that there are any other rules. Not ones that matter.

Neil Gaiman

Writing has laws of perspective, of light and shade just as painting does, or music. If you are born knowing them, fine, if not, learn them. Then rearrange the rules to suit yourself.

Truman Capote

To write well, express yourself like the common people think, but think like a wise man.

Aristotle

A little talent is a good thing to have if you want to be a writer. But the only real requirement is the ability to remember every scar.

Stephen King

Fiction writing is a strange business when you think about it. You sit down and weave a network of lies to explore deeper truths.

Wally Lamb

Writing's funny. It's like walking down a hall in the dark looking for the light switch, and suddenly you find it, flip it on, and then you discover the hallway you passed through is papered with the novel you've written.

Jonathan Safran Foer

There are three rules for writing a novel. Unfortunately, no one knows what they are.

W. Somerset Maugham

Writing, like life itself, is a voyage of discovery.

Henry Miller

End with an image and don't explain.

Stanley Kunitz

Focus on the story, not the sentence.

James Patterson

To get the right word in the right place is a rare achievement.

Mark Twain

A writer should concern himself with
whatever absorbs his fancy, stirs his heart, and
unlimbers his typewriter. A writer has the duty
to be good, not lousy; true, not false; lively,
not dull; accurate, not full of error. He should
tend to lift people up, not lower them down.
Writers do not merely reflect and interpret
life, they inform and shape life.

E. B. White

When you are describing
A shape, or sound, or tint,
Don't state the matter plainly,
But put it in a hint;
And learn to look at all things
With a sort of mental squint.

Lewis Carroll

If the writing is honest, it cannot be separated
from the person who wrote it.

Tennessee Williams

Writing is a job, a talent, but it's also the place
to go in your head. It is the imaginary friend
you drink your tea with in the afternoon.

Ann Patchett

You're learning to write a book every time you sit down to do it. I know that sounds a little strange, but in every book you're presented with new possibilities, new environment, different people, new story lines. You're learning how to do it all over again.

Carol O'Connell

The author should use the right word, not its second cousin.

Mark Twain

The job of the artist is always to deepen the mystery.

Francis Bacon

A novel is like a bow, and the violin that produces the sound is the reader's soul.

Stendhal

The best work that anybody ever writes is the work that is on the verge of embarrassing him, always.

Arthur Miller

As a writer you should not judge. You should understand.

Ernest Hemingway

Use all your senses, but don't get weird about it. When writing descriptively, don't forget the senses other than sight. Describe sounds, smells, tastes, and textures too, but only when it adds meaningfully to the description.

Brian Wasko

It is a great privilege to make one's living from writing sentences. The sentence is the greatest invention of civilization … The great thrill is when a sentence that starts out being completely plain suddenly begins to sing, rising far above itself and above any expectation I might have had for it.

John Banville

– Never use a metaphor, simile, or other figure of speech which you are used to seeing in print.
– Never use a long word where a short one will do.
– If it is possible to cut a word out, always cut it out.
– Never use the passive where you can use the active.
– Never use a foreign phrase, a scientific word, or a jargon word if you can think of an everyday English equivalent.

– Break any of these rules sooner than say anything outright barbarous.

George Orwell

Get it down. Take chances. It may be bad, but it's the only way you can do anything really good.

William Faulkner

Be courageous and try to write in a way that scares you a little.

Holley Gerth

Always go with the choice that scares you the most, because that's the one that is going to help you grow.

Caroline Myss

Every book is three books, after all; the one the writer intended, the one the reader expected, and the one that casts its shadow when the first two meet by moonlight.

John W. Ford

Talent is helpful in writing, but guts are absolutely essential.

Jessamyn West

Put it before them briefly so they will read it,

clearly so they will appreciate it, picturesquely
so they will remember it, and above all,
accurately so they will be guided by its light.

Joseph Pulitzer

Whenever you write, whatever you write,
never make the mistake of assuming the
audience is any less intelligent than you are.

Rod Serling

Not only is your story worth telling, but it can
be told in words so painstakingly eloquent
that it becomes a song.

Gloria Naylor

Write the kind of story you would like to read.
People will give you all sorts of advice about
writing, but if you are not writing something
you like, no one else will like it either.

Meg Cabot

One always has a better book in one's mind
than one can manage to get onto paper.

Michael Cunningham

A good novel tells us the truth about its hero;
but a bad novel tells us the truth about its
author.

G.K. Chesterton

The only way you can write the truth is to assume that what you set down will never be read. Not by any other person, and not even by yourself at some later date. Otherwise you begin excusing yourself. You must see the writing as emerging like a long scroll of ink from the index finger of your right hand; you must see your left hand erasing it.

Margaret Atwood

Normally, in anything I do, I'm fairly miserable. I do it, and I get grumpy because there is a huge, vast gulf, this aching disparity, between the platonic ideal of the project that was living in my head, and the small, sad, wizened, shaking, squeaking thing that I actually produce.

Neil Gaiman

I have spent a good many years since—too many, I think—being ashamed about what I write. I think I was forty before I realized that almost every writer of fiction or poetry who has ever published a line has been accused by someone of wasting his or her God-given talent. If you write (or paint or dance or sculpt or sing, I suppose), someone will try to make you feel lousy about it, that's all.

Stephen King

Writers don't write from experience, although many are hesitant to admit that they don't. If you wrote from experience, you'd get maybe one book, maybe three poems. Writers write from empathy.

Nikki Giovanni

Don't tell me the moon is shining; show me the glint of light on broken glass.

Anton Chekhov

You must write for yourself and not what you think people want to read.

Jodi Ellen Malpas

A good story should make you laugh, and a moment later break your heart.

Chuck Palahniuk

The secret of being a writer: not to expect others to value what you've done as you value it, not to expect anyone else to perceive in it the emotions you have invested in it. Once this is understood, all will be well.

Joyce Carol Oates

I think that everything you do helps you to write if you're a writer. Adversity and success both contribute largely to making you what you are. If you don't experience either one of those, you're being deprived of something.

Shelby Foote

Writing, like life itself, is a voyage of discovery.

Henry Miller

To get the right word in the right place is a rare achievement.

Mark Twain

The writer must be in it. He can't be to one side of it, ever. He has to be endangered by it. His own attitudes have to be tested in it. The best work that anybody ever writes is the work that is on the verge of embarrassing him, always.

Arthur Miller

I know nothing in the world that has as much power as a word. Sometimes I write one, and I look at it, until it begins to shine.

Emily Dickinson

People may forget the plot of a beloved book, they may forget many of its scenes and characters, but people will never forget how it made them feel or the lessons it taught them.

Ana-Carolina Pereira

End with an image and don't explain.

Stanley Kunitz

Focus on the story, not the sentence.

James Patterson

Use plain, simple language, short words and brief sentences. That is the way to write English—it is the modern way and the best way. Stick to it; don't let fluff and flowers and verbosity creep in.

Mark Twain

Increase your word power. Words are the raw material of our craft. The greater your vocabulary the more effective your writing. We who write in English are fortunate to have the richest and most versatile language in the world. Respect it.

P. D. James

Learn the rules like a pro so you can break them like an artist.

Pablo Picasso

Be courageous and try to write in a way that scares you a little.

Holley Gerth

Not only is your story worth telling, but it can be told in words so painstakingly eloquent that it becomes a song.

Gloria Naylor

Write the kind of story you would like to read. People will give you all sorts of advice about writing, but if you are not writing something you like, no one else will like it either.

Meg Cabot

I try to leave out the parts that people skip.

Elmore Leonard

Tell the readers a story! Because without a story, you are merely using words to prove you can string them together in logical sentences.

Anne McCaffrey

Don't say you were a bit confused and sort of tired and a little depressed and somewhat annoyed. Be tired. Be confused. Be depressed. Be annoyed. Don't hedge your prose with little timidities. Good writing is lean and confident.

William Zinsser

Don't use adjectives which merely tell us how you want us to feel about the thing you are describing. I mean, instead of telling us a thing was "terrible," describe it so that we'll be terrified. Don't say it was "delightful"; make us say "delightful when we're read the description.

C. S. Lewis

Move the reader, make them happy and sad and excited and scared. Make them stare into space after they've put the book down, thinking about the tale that's become a part of them.

James Dashner

The idea is to write it so that people hear it and it slides through the brain and goes straight to the heart.

Maya Angelou

When you catch an adjective, kill it. No, I don't mean utterly, but kill most of them— then the rest will be valuable. They weaken when they are close together. They give strength when they are wide apart. An adjective habit, or a wordy, diffuse, flowery habit, once fastened upon a person, is as hard to get rid of as any other vice.

Mark Twain

Writers should begin their stories with the event that kicks off the story, and then spoon-feed us background information only when it's needed to understand what's going on.

Evan Marshall

Be an unstoppable force. Write with an imaginary machete strapped to your thigh. This is not wishy-washy, polite, drinking-tea-with-your-pinkie-sticking-out stuff. It's who you want to be, your most powerful self. Write your books. Finish them, then make them better. Find the way. No one will make this dream come true for you but you.

Laini Taylor

The most original authors are not so because they advance what is new, but because they put what they have to say as if it had never been said before.

Johann Wolfgang von Goethe

The bigger the issue, the smaller you write.

Remember that. You don't write about the horrors of war. No. You write about a kid's burnt socks lying on the road. You pick the smallest manageable part of the big thing, and you work off the resonance.

Richard Price

At the beginning of their careers many writers have a need to overwrite. They choose carefully turned-out phrases; they want to impress their readers with their large vocabularies. By the excesses of their language, these young men and women try to hide their sense of inexperience. With maturity the writer becomes more secure in his ideas. He finds his real tone and develops a simple and effective style.

Jorge Luis Borges

I can't remember how many times I advised students to stop writing the sunny hours and write from where it hurts. No one wants to read polite. It puts them to sleep.

Anne Bernays

Good writers are those who keep the language efficient. That is to say, keep it accurate, keep it clear.

Ezra Pound

When speaking aloud, you punctuate constantly—with body language. Your listener hears commas, dashes, question marks, exclamation points, quotation marks as you shout, whisper, pause, wave your arms, roll your eyes, wrinkle your brow. In writing, punctuation plays the role of body language. It helps readers hear you the way you want to be heard.

Russell Baker

The secret of good writing is to strip every sentence to its cleanest components. Every word that serves no function, every long word that could be a short word, every adverb that carries the same meaning that's already in the verb … these are the thousand and one adulterants that weaken the strengthen of a sentence.

William Zinsser

Bear in mind, when you're choosing your words and stringing them together, how they sound. his may seem absurd: readers read with their eyes. But in fact they hear what they are reading far more than you realize.

William Zinsser

Every successful piece of nonfiction should

leave the reader with one provocative thought that he or she didn't have before. Not two thoughts, or five—just one. So decide what single point you want to leave in the reader's mind.

William Zinsser

A scrupulous writer, in every sentence that he writes, will ask himself at least four questions, thus:
1. What am I trying to say?
2. What words will express it?
3. What image or idiom will make it clearer?
4. Is this image fresh enough to have an effect?

George Orwell

If you are using dialog—say it aloud as you write it. Only then will it have the sound of speech.

John Steinbeck

A short story must have a single mood and every sentence must build towards it.

Edgar Allen Poe

If you do not hear music in your words, you

have put too much thought into your writing
and not enough heart.

Terry Brooks

Write from the heart as well as the head.
Write about what makes you angry, what
moves you to tears, the things about which
you feel passionately. If you feel it when you
write, others will feel it when they read.

Malorie Blackman

What I like in a good author is not what he
says, but what he whispers.

Logan Pearsall Smith

Look back upstream. If you have come to
your planned ending and it doesn't seem to be
working, run your eye up the page and the
page before that. You may see that your best
ending is somewhere in there, that you were
finished before you thought you were.

John McPhee

The simpler you say it, the more eloquent it is.

August Wilson

One day I will find the right words, and they
will be simple.

Jack Kerouac

9

Where Do I Get Fresh Ideas?

If you are having trouble getting started, look out the window. The whole world is a story, and every moment is a miracle.

Bruce Taylor

I would tell aspiring writers to observe. They already know it is vital to read and write whenever possible, but often people forget to watch what is going on every day in their surroundings. That is where your ideas come from. Keep one eye on your computer screen and the other on the world around you.

Eoin Colfer

Everybody walks past a thousand story ideas every day. The good writers are the ones who see five or six of them. Most people don't see any.

Orson Scott Card

My inspiration tends to come from two words. The two most important words to a writer: "What if?"

Beth Revis

An idea, like a ghost, must be spoken to a little before it will explain itself.

Charles Dickens

Writers see the world differently. Every voice we hear, every face we see, every hand we touch could become story fabric.

Buffy Andrews

Writers end up writing about their obsessions. Things that haunt them; things they can't forget; stories they carry in their bodies waiting to be released.

Natalie Goldberg

If a writer stops observing he is finished. Experience is communicated by small details intimately observed.

Ernest Hemingway

Don't try to figure out what other people want to hear from you; figure out what you have to say. It's the one and only thing you have to offer.

Barbara Kingsolver

It's very important to write things down instantly, or you can lose the way you were thinking out a line. I have a rule that if I wake up at 3 in the morning and think of something, I write it down. I can't wait until morning—it'll be gone.

Mary Oliver

We are writers, and we never ask one another where we get our ideas; we know we don't know.

Stephen King

From the simplest lyric to the most complex novel, literature is asking us to pay attention. Pay attention to the frog. Pay attention to the west wind. Pay attention to the boy on the raft, the lady on the tower, the old man on the train … pay attention to the world and all that dwells therein.

Frederick Buechner

Don't forget—no one else sees the world the way you do, so no one else can tell the stories that you have to tell.

Charles de Lint

Fill your paper with the breathings of your heart.

William Wordsworth

Nothing that ever happens to a novelist is ever wasted.

P. D. James

There's always something to write about. If there's not then you need to live life more aggressively.

Min Kim

You own everything that happened to you. Tell your stories. If people wanted you to write warmly about them, they should've behaved better.

Anne Lamott

Write about what disturbs you, what you fear, what you have not been willing to speak about. Be willing to be split open.

Natalie Goldberg

There's no subject you don't have permission to write about.

William Zinsser

One of the few things I know about writing is this: spend it all, shoot it, play it, lose it, all, right away, every time. Do not hoard what seems good for a later place … Something more will arise for later, something better.

Annie Dillard

And above all, watch with glittering eyes the whole world around you because the greatest secrets are always hidden in the most unlikely places. Those who don't believe in magic will never find it.

Roald Dahl

Inspiration usually comes during work, rather than before it.

Madeline L'Engle

Writers see the world differently. Every voice we hear, every face we see, every hand we touch could become story fabric.

Buffy Andrews

Imagine what you are writing about. See it and live it. Do not think it up laboriously, as if you were working out mental arithmetic. Just look at it, touch it, smell it, listen to it, turn yourself into it. When you do this, the words look after themselves, like magic.

Ted Hughes

I just write what I wanted to write. I write what amuses me. It's totally for myself.

J. K. Rowling

I didn't set out to write this book. It crept up on me when I wasn't looking, when I didn't know I was writing it.

Mark David Gerson

Honing your ability to observe accurately— and to write down what you've noticed— must be part of your lifelong commitment to fiction.

Jack M. Bickham

If you're going to be a writer, the first essential is just to write. Do not wait for an idea. Start writing something and the ideas will come. You have to turn the faucet on before the water starts to flow.

Louis L'Amour

Many times I just sit for three hours with no ideas coming to me. But I know one thing: if an idea does come between nine and twelve, I am there ready for it.

Flannery O'Connor

Put your heart and soul on the page.

Victoria Zachheim

Keep a diary, but don't just list all the things you did during the day. Pick one incident and write it up as a brief vignette. Give it color, include quotes and dialog, shape it like a story with a beginning, middle and end—as if it were a short story or an episode in a novel. It's great practice. Do this while figuring out what you want to write a book about. The book may even emerge from within this running diary.

John Berendt

The best time for planning a book is while

you're doing the dishes.

Agatha Christie

You get ideas from daydreaming. You get ideas from being bored. You get ideas all the time. The only difference between writers and other people is we notice when we're doing it.

Neil Gaiman

Let's get one thing clear right now, shall we? There is no Idea Dump, no Story Central, no Island of the Buried Bestsellers; good story ideas seem to come quite literally from nowhere, sailing at you right out of the empty sky: two previously unrelated ideas come together and make something new under the sun. Your job isn't to find these ideas but to recognize them when they show up.

Stephen King

All words are pegs to hang ideas on.

Henry Ward Beecher

Get a good idea and stay with it. Dog it and work at it until it's done, and done right.

Walt Disney

A good writer is always a people watcher.

Judy Blume

A writer lives, at best, in a state of
astonishment. Beneath any feeling he has of
the good or evil of the world lies a deeper one
of wonder at it all.

William Sansom

Creativity is piercing the mundane to find the
marvelous.

Bill Moyers

The discipline of the writer is to learn to be
still and listen to what his subject has to tell
him.

Rachel Carson

You must write it all out, at any cost. Writing
is thinking. It is more than living, for it is
being conscious of living.

Anne Morrow Lindbergh

A book is a device to ignite the imagination.

Alan Bennett

What doesn't kill us gives us something new
to write about.

Julie Wright

The idea of just wandering off to a café with a
notebook and writing and seeing where that

takes me for a while is just bliss.

J. K. Rowling

Most writers spend their lives standing a little apart from the crowd, watching and listening and hoping to catch that tiny hint of despair, that sliver of malice, that makes them think, "Aha, here is a story."

Ayelet Waldman

Inspiration usually comes during work, rather than before it.

Madeline L'Engle

Everybody walks past a thousand story ideas every day. The good writers are the ones who see five or six of them. Most people don't see any.

Orson Scott Card

What people are ashamed of usually makes a good story.

F. Scott Fitzgerald

The deeper you can listen, the better you can write.

Natalie Goldberg

To write, you need to find what you love.

D. J. McHale

Happiness for me is getting to write about the most important things I know.

Richard Ford

Novels begin, not on the page, but in meditation and day-dreaming—in thinking, not writing.

Joyce Carol Oates

But with writers, there's nothing wrong with melancholy. It's an important color in writing.

Paul McCartney

I think that everything you do helps you to write if you're a writer. Adversity and success both contribute largely to making you what you are. If you don't experience either one of those, you're being deprived of something.

Shelby Foote

The secret of it all, is to write in the gush, the throb, the flood, of the moment—to put things down without deliberation—without worrying about their style—without waiting for a fit time or place. I always worked that way. I took the first scrap of paper, the first doorstep, the first desk, and wrote—wrote, wrote … By writing at the instant the very heartbeat of life is caught.

Walt Whitman

And by the way, everything in life is writable about if you have the outgoing guts to do it, and the imagination to improvise. The worst enemy to creativity is self-doubt.

Sylvia Plath

A writer's job is to imagine everything so personally that the fiction is as vivid as memories.

John Irving

Live your life as a curious person. Try to see the entire world as your muse. Ask questions. Dismiss nothing. Eavesdrop. Always eavesdrop. You'll have more fun, learn all the time, and when the time comes to sit down and write, you'll have a whole line-up of stories just waiting to be told.

Lauren Kate

Following that scavenger hunt of curiosity can lead you to amazing, unexpected places.

Elizabeth Gilbert

Whether you want to entertain or to provoke, to break hearts or reassure them, what you bring to your writing must consist of your longings and disappointments.

Rafael Yglesias

Imagine what you are writing about. See it and live it. Do not think it up laboriously, as if you were working out mental arithmetic. Just look at it, touch it, smell it, listen to it, turn yourself into it. When you do this, the words look after themselves, like magic.

Ted Hughes

You can't wait for inspiration. You have to go after it with a club.

Jack London

Ideas aren't magical; the only tricky part is holding on to one long enough to get it written down.

Lynn Abbey

Writing students can be great at producing a single page of well-crafted prose; what they sometimes lack is the ability to take the reader on a journey, with all the changes of terrain, speed and mood that a long journey involves. Most novels will want to move close, linger,

move back, move on, in pretty cinematic
ways.

Sarah Waters

You get ideas from daydreaming. You get
ideas from being bored. You get ideas all the
time. The only difference between writers and
other people is we notice when we're doing it.

Neil Gaiman

Inspiration comes of working every day.

Charles Baudelaire

There's always something to write about. If
there's not then you need to live life more
aggressively.

Min Kim

Inspiration is everywhere. Carry a notebook.

Victor Hugo

The creations of a great writer are little more
than the moods and passions of his own
heart, given surnames and Christian names,
and sent to walk the earth.

William Butler Yeats

Writing is a job, a talent, but it's also the place

to go in your head. It is the imaginary friend
you drink your tea with in the afternoon.

Ann Patchett

Write loads, read voraciously, go out and live.
Things will emerge in the spaces in between
and you might be surprised by what does.

Irenosen Okojie

Writers see the world differently. Every voice
we hear, every face we see, every hand we
touch could become story fabric.

Buffy Andrews

Writers end up writing about their obsessions.
Things that haunt them; things they can't
forget; stories they carry in their bodies
waiting to be released.

Natalie Goldberg

Open your mind to new experiences,
particularly to the study of other people.
Nothing that ever happens to a writer—
however happy, however tragic—is ever
wasted.

P.D. James

If a writer stops observing he is finished.
Experience is communicated by small details

intimately observed.

Ernest Hemingway

It's very important to write things down instantly, or you can lose the way you were thinking out a line. I have a rule that if I wake up at 3 in the morning and think of something, I write it down. I can't wait until morning—it'll be gone.

Mary Oliver

A writer lives, at best, in a state of astonishment. Beneath any feeling he has of the good or evil of the world lies a deeper one of wonder at it all.

William Sansom

Keep a diary, but don't just list all the things you did during the day. Pick one incident and write it up as a brief vignette. Give it color, include quotes and dialog, shape it like a story with a beginning, middle and end—as if it were a short story or an episode in a novel. It's great practice. Do this while figuring out what you want to write a book about. The book may even emerge from within this running diary.

John Berendt

Bad things don't happen to writers; it's all material.

Garrison Keillor

And above all, watch with glittering eyes the whole world around you because the greatest secrets are always hidden in the most unlikely places. Those who don't believe in magic will never find it.

Roald Dahl

Don't loaf and invite inspiration; light out after it with a club, and if you don't get it you will nonetheless get something that looks remarkable like it.

Jack London

Don't forget—no one else sees the world the way you do, so no one else can tell the stories that you have to tell.

Charles de Lint

Fill your paper with the breathings of your heart.

William Wordsworth

There's no subject you don't have permission to write about.

William Zinsser

One of the few things I know about writing is this: spend it all, shoot it, play it, lose it, all, right away, every time. Do not hoard what seems good for a later place … Something more will arise for later, something better.

Annie Dillard

At night, when the objective world has slunk back into its cavern and left dreamers to their own, there come inspirations and capabilities impossible at any less magical and quiet hour. No one knows whether or not he is a writer unless he has tried writing at night.

H.P. Lovecraft

Write down everything that comes to you in an adrenalin rush in the small hours, and on waking up. About one-half—truly—will turn out to be useful and it sets you up for the morning work.

Laura Cumming

Your intuition knows what to write, so get out of the way.

Ray Bradbury

10
Developing The Plot

Literature was not born the day when a boy crying "wolf, wolf" came running out of the Neanderthal valley with a big gray wolf at his heels; literature was born on the day when a boy came crying "wolf, wolf" and there was no wolf behind him.

Vladimir Nabokov

An opening line should invite the reader to begin the story. It should say: Listen. Come in here. You want to know about this.

Stephen King

Remember: plot is no more than footprints left in the snow after your characters have run by on their way to incredible destinations.

Ray Bradbury

If any scene you're writing feels bland and boring, go back and make sure you've used all five senses.

Jean Marie Stine

I get annoyed when a self-indulgent writer just shows off what he knows but doesn't really tell a story. To me storytelling is first a craft. Then if you're lucky, it becomes an art form. But first, it's got to be a craft. You've got to have a beginning, middle and end.

Robert Ludlum

Novels are forged in passion, demand fidelity and commitment, often drive you to boredom or rage, sleep with you at night. They are the long haul. They are marriage. Stories, on the other hand, you can lose yourself in for a few weeks and then wrap up, or grow tired of and abandon and (maybe) return to later. They can cuddle you sweetly, or make you get on your knees and beg.

David Leavitt

To uncover the plot of your story, don't ask what should happen, but what should go wrong. To uncover the meaning of your story, don't ask what the theme is, but rather, what is discovered. Characters making choices to resolve tension—that's your plot. If your protagonist has no goal, makes no choices, has no struggle to overcome, you have no plot.

Steven James

In Act 1, get your character up in a tree; in Act 2, throw stones at them; and in Act 3, get them down again.

George M. Cohan

Stories may well be lies, but they are good lies that say true things, and which can sometimes pay the rent.

Neil Gaiman

But how could you live and have no story to tell?

Fyodor Dostoyevsky

Good writing is remembering detail. Most people want to forget. Don't forget things

that were painful or embarrassing or silly.
Turn them into a story that tells the truth.

Paul Danziger

In order to have a plot, you have to have a
conflict. Something bad has to happen.

Mike Judge

I think every writer stands in the doorway of
their prison. Half in, half out. The very act of
storytelling is a return to the prison of what
torments us and keeps us captive, and writers
are repeat offenders.

Sherman Alexie

In the planning stages of a book, don't plan
the ending. It has to be earned by all that will
go before it.

Rose Tremain

One of the biggest, and possibly the biggest,
obstacle to becoming a writer … is learning to
live with the fact that the wonderful story in
your head is infinitely better, truer, more
moving, more fascinating, more perceptive,
than anything you're going to manage to get
down on paper.

Robin McKinley

Obstacles. Conflict. Pain and suffering. Sometimes, being stuck on a story is just because things are too easy.

Chuck Wendig

One KEY way to keep the momentum going is to constantly have unanswered questions.

Jody Hedlund

Good books don't give up all their secrets at once.

Stephen King

Always mystify, torture, mislead, and surprise the audience as much as possible.

Don Roff

Write down every question that comes to mind, whether you plan to answer them right away or not, or even if the question seems irrelevant. What you're doing is making a list of prompts specifically for your story.

Alina Sandor

I still approach each book with the same basic plan in mind—to put some people under severe stress and see how they hold up.

Terry Brooks

Be prepared to discover that the story is not going to be exactly how you pictured it. I think that is one of the most exciting things about writing – enjoy it!

Wendy Orr

Even if you plot your books, sometimes you won't know what is coming until the words appear on the page. Something happens when you commit to the page, to the word count goal and you write through the frustration and the annoyance and the self-criticism. Creativity emerges.

Joanna Penn

If you've been studying the craft, you'll naturally be inclined to show more than tell, write snappy dialogue, and be aware of how much backstory you're allowing in. That's great. But don't let yourself get caught up in those details. Keep the forward momentum going.

Rachelle Gardner

The pages are still blank, but there is a miraculous feeling of the words being there, written in invisible ink and clamoring to become visible.

Vladimir Nabokov

There's always room for a story that can transport people to another place.

J. K. Rowling

There are some books that refuse to be written. They stand their ground year after year and will not be persuaded. It isn't because the book is not there and worth being written — it is only because the right form of the story does not present itself. There is only one right form for a story and if you fail to find that form the story will not tell itself.

Mark Twain

Honing your ability to observe accurately— and to write down what you've noticed— must be part of your lifelong commitment to fiction.

Jack M. Bickham

I don't want to write that first sentence until all the important connections in the novel are known to me. As if the story has already taken place, and it's my responsibility to put it in the right order to tell it to you.

John Irving

The most difficult part of any crime novel is the plotting. It all begins simply enough, but soon you're dealing with a multitude of linked characters, strands, themes and red herrings—and you need to try to control these unruly elements and weave them into a pattern.

Ian Rankin

You must understand that when you are writing a novel you are not making anything up. It's all there and you just have to find it.

Thomas Harris

The reason that fiction is more interesting than any other form of literature, to those who really like to study people, is that in fiction the author can really tell the truth without humiliating himself.

Eleanor Roosevelt

No one says a novel has to be one thing. It can be anything it wants to be, a vaudeville show, the six o'clock news, the mumblings of wild men saddled by demons.

Ishmael Reed

A good story is always more dazzling than a broken piece of truth.

Diane Setterfield

If a story is not about the hearer, he will not

listen. And here I make a rule—a great and interesting story is about everyone or it will not last.

John Steinbeck

Description begins in the writer's imagination, but should finish in the reader's.

Stephen King

Plot is people. Human emotions and desires founded on the realities of life, working at cross purposes, getting hotter and fiercer as they strike against each other until finally there's an explosion—that's plot.

Leigh Brackett

In the inmost cave where we are most afraid to enter is where the greatest treasure lies.

Joseph Campbell

When you emphasize the opposite of what's really going to happen, you not only keep readers from guessing the true course of events, you also achieve a subtle kind of foreshadowing.

K. M. Weiland

Make up a story ... for our sake and yours forget your name in the street; tell us what the world has been to you in the dark places and in the light. Don't tell us what to believe, what to fear. Show us belief's wide skirt and the stitch that unravels fear's caul.

Toni Morrison

I think of my novels as being something like fairground rides: my job is to strap the reader into their car at the start of chapter one, then trundle and whiz them through scenes and surprises, on a carefully planned route, and at a finely engineered pace.

Sarah Waters

There's a story behind anything. How a picture got on a wall. How a scar got on your face. Sometimes the stories are simple, and sometimes they are hard and heart-breaking.

Mitch Albom

The cat sat on the mat is not a story. The cat sat on the other cat's mat is a story.

John le Carre

Think of your book in layers. The first layer will by its nature be rough—it's just a sketch—so don't get frustrated if it feels too light or is badly drawn. You'll add to your story as you go, layering more character, deeper plot, better description, and twists and turns; and painting in light and shade.

Abie Longstaff

A good novelist does not create events, he watches them happen and then writes down what he sees.

Stephen King

Each thing you add to your story is a drop of paint falling into clear water; it spreads through and colors everything.

Lisa Cron

A story isn't a charcoal sketch, where every stroke lies on the surface to be seen. It's an oil painting, filled with layers that the author must uncover so carefully to show its beauty.

Amelia Atwater-Rhodes

It's funny … how often I seem to build a story around one sentence, nearly always the last one, too.

Daphne du Maurier

A good story cannot be devised; it has to be distilled.

Raymond Chandler

When I get an idea for a book I spend a lot of time thinking about the plot and characters before I write a word.

Philip Margolin

People have forgotten how to tell a story. Stories don't have a middle or an end any more. They usually have a beginning that never stops beginning.

Steven Spielberg

When the reader and one narrator know something the other narrator does not, the opportunities for suspense and plot development and the shifting of reader sympathies get really interesting.

Sara Zarr

When you're writing, the most important thing, your north star, is the ending. Every word you write should be weighed against that, and if it isn't contributing to your ending, it's a sideline and should be omitted.

Raymond E. Feist

11

Developing The Characters

It begins with a character, usually, and once he stands up on his feet and begins to move, all I can do is trot along behind him with a paper and a pencil trying to keep up long enough to put down what he says and does.

William Faulkner

Over and over I feel as if my characters know who they are and what happens to them and where they have been and where they will go and what they are capable of doing but they need me to write it down for them because their handwriting is so bad.

Anne Lamott

Let your characters speak. Don't tell us what they said.

Amanda Patterson

If you're silent for a long time, people just arrive in your mind.

Alice Walker

The poor novelist constructs his characters: he controls them and makes them speak. The true novelist listens to them and watches them function: he eavesdrops on them even before he knows them.

Andre Gide

These characters in my mind are not real. They aren't. When a character puts me under house arrest, I have to remember that I can escape.

Michael Cadnum

When plot flags, bring in a man with a gun.

Raymond Chandler

You can't blame a writer for what the characters say.

Truman Capote

It's true that it's a solitary occupation, but you

would be surprised at how much companionship a group of imaginary characters can offer once you get to know them.

Anne Tyler

Treat all your secondary characters like they think the book's about them.

Jocelyn Hughes

Show, don't tell. In other words, don't write that a character behaved badly; show us their bad behavior instead.

Marina Lewycka

The most important things to remember about back story are that (a) everyone has a history and (b) most of it isn't very interesting.

Stephen King

If you're struggling with writing a character, write 20 things that the reader will never know about your character. These will naturally bleed into your writing and provide a richness even though you don't share the detail.

Barbara Poelle

I'm not one of those people who as a writer

lets my characters tell me what they want to do or call to me or seek me. I go seeking for things, using them as an agent, really.

Richard Ford

All kinds of information about your main character will come up while you're writing your first draft. Maybe she lives in a noisy apartment building. Or her mom is a gung-ho Amway seller. Or her next door neighbor is recuperating from a terrible accident. Or she feels a deep hatred for Smurfs. This stuff will spill out in your first chapters. Let it.

Anne R. Allen

When in doubt, make trouble for your character. Don't let her stand on the edge of the pool, dipping her toe. Come up behind her and give her a good hard shove. That's my advice to you now. Make trouble for your character. In life we try to avoid trouble. We chew on our choices endlessly. We go to shrinks, we talk to our friends. In fiction, this is deadly. Protagonists need to screw up, act impulsively, have enemies, get into trouble.

Janet Fitch

Be unkind to your characters when you are

exploring who they are. Challenge them, put them in difficult situations and see how they respond, present them with strong choices and show us their development. Interrogate them. Do they have any transgressions? Once you see the world from your characters' point of view, their emotional logic will be authentic.

Jenny Downham

The writer's job is to get the main character up a tree, and then once he's up there, throw rocks at him.

Vladimir Nabokov

I have to ruin my character's life, and I have to make that ruination believable, engaging, satisfying and surprising.

David Corbett

Your characters, if you want them to be interesting, can't win all the time. They have to fail as well. But they can't just fail. The trick is to get them to fail because of an inner conflict.

Karen Woodward

I put ordinary people in jeopardy and give them the opportunity to be heroic. Then there's a great payoff for the reader at the end, when the heroic character gets what he or she deserves. Readers will come back again and again if they feel satisfied at the end.

Terri Blackstock

I always suspect characters who are painted as lovely, decent human beings. I would always question where the darkness lies.

Martin McDonagh

Coincidences to get characters into trouble are great; coincidences to get them out of it are cheating.

Emma Coats

If a character wants to go in a direction you hadn't anticipated, by all means go check it out. See where that scary road leads. It might lead to a better story. It might lead to fixing a problem you had earlier (or will run into later) in the story. Or it could be a dead end. But guess what, dead ends are okay. Dead ends make you a better writer. Just go back the way you came and find a new route.

Cris Freese

A character with one or more secrets adds

mystery and intrigue to any genre.

Linda S. Clare

The personages in a tale shall be alive, except in the case of corpses, and that always the reader shall be able to tell the corpses from the others.

Mark Twain

The author shall make the reader feel a deep interest in the personages of his tale and their fate; and that he shall make the reader love the good people in the tale and hate the bad ones.

Mark Twain

Strangely enough, the first character in Fried Green Tomatoes was the café, and the town. I think a place can be as much a character in a novel as the people.

Fannie Flagg

Don't say the old lady screamed. Bring her on and let her scream.

Mark Twain

A writer has to have an imagination—that's what makes a writer. He has to be able to put himself imaginatively in the position of whatever character he selects.

W. R. Burnett

If you are using dialogue, say it aloud as you write it. Only then will it have the sound of speech.

John Steinbeck

Only a writer will hold conversations with people that don't exist. We don't talk to ourselves …we talk to people we created from nothing.

Joseph Eastwood

When writing a novel a writer should create living people; people not characters. A character is a caricature.

Ernest Hemingway

When reading, we don't fall in love with the characters' appearance. We fall in love with their words, their thoughts, and their hearts. We fall in love with their souls.

Unknown

Every character should want something, even if it's only a glass of water.

Kurt Vonnegut

Be clear on every character's agenda in a scene, and the agendas in conflict. Before you write take just a moment to jot down what each character in the scene wants, even if (as Kurt Vonnegut once said) it is only a glass of water.

James Scott Bell

The characters in a tale should be so clearly defined that the reader can tell beforehand what each will do in a given emergency.

Mark Twain

Ideally, in every scene each character brings out qualities that mark the dimensions of the others. All are held in constellation by the weight of the protagonist at the center.

Robert McKee

You don't really understand an antagonist until you understand why he's a protagonist in his own version of the world.

John Rogers

Which of us has not felt that the character we are reading in the printed page is more real than the person standing beside us?

Cornelia Funke

Whenever you create a minor character, figure out a way to use his strengths and weaknesses to compare or contrast with your protagonist.

K. M. Weiland

Over and over I feel as if my characters know who they are and what happens to them and where they have been and where they will go and what they are capable of doing, but they need me to write it down for them because their handwriting is so bad.

Anne Lamott

We are not seduced by plots. We are seduced by characters.

Guy Gallo

The novels I remember best have empathetic characters whose motivations I understand— even if I don't agree with them—and a plot that I can't stop thinking about. The best novels make me think—what could happen, and what would I do if it happened to me?

Amanda Peterson

I like to think of what happens to characters in good novels and stories as knots—things keep knotting up. And by the end of the story, readers see an unknotting of sorts.

Terry McMillan

When you know your characters inside out, when you know what makes them really "comfortable," throw the exact opposite at them and observe how they cope. It's only when we are met with challenges that our true self comes to the fore, and this is the really interesting stuff, for it's simple and honest warts-and-all reality.

Tracey Corderoy

The writer is both a sadist and a masochist. We create people we love, and then we torture them. The more we love them, and the more cleverly we torture them along the lines of their greatest vulnerability and fear, the better the story.

Janet Fitch

By the end, you should be inside your character, actually operating from within somebody else, and knowing him pretty well, as that person knows himself or herself. You're sort of a predator, an invader of people.

William Trevor

The goal, I suppose, any fiction writer has, no matter what your subject, is to hit the human heart and the tear ducts and the nape of the neck and to make a person feel something about what the characters are going through and to experience the moral paradoxes and struggles of being human.

Tim O'Brien

Your minor characters don't know that they're minor characters. They are more than capable of impacting the story in a big way.

Ryan Reudell

Authors also create lovable, friendly characters, then proceed to do terrible things to them, like throw them in unsightly librarian-controlled dungeons. This makes readers feel hurt and worried for the characters. The simple truth is that authors like making people squirm. If this weren't the case, all novels would be filled completely with cute bunnies having birthday parties.

Brandon Sanderson

Character is the very life of fiction. Setting exists so that the character has someplace to stand. Plot exists so the character can discover what he is really like, forcing the character to choice and action. And theme exists only to make the character stand up and be somebody.

John Gardner

The art of the novel is to arrive at that artless point where your characters become more real than yourself.

Norman Mailer

As you write, take a moment after finishing each scene and make sure you know what your main character is feeling. And then ask yourself if the audience needs to see what she's feeling.

Kristina Reed

You are going to love some of your characters, because they are you or some facet of you, and you are going to hate some of your characters for the same reason.

Anne Lamott

Love your characters into existence.

Patricia Lee Gauch

A good novelist does not lead his characters, he follows them.

Stephen King

All characters are based on elements of a
writer's personal experience.

Robert Holdstock

To make characters convincing, you have to
get right inside their heads and experience the
world as they do. You have to be them and
use their senses accordingly, whether they are
human, animal or alien.

Chris d'Lacey

Dialog is not just quotation. It is grimaces,
pauses, adjustments of blouse buttons,
doodles on a napkin, and crossings of legs.

Jerome Stern

Ask: What does my character want? For me
that is the single most important question to
ask when writing a novel. I need my main
character to want something very badly, and I
need to understand completely and utterly
what it is. That's because this thing, or tangle
of things, will become the driving force of the
book.

Sue Monk Kidd

Find out what your hero or heroine wants,
and when he or she wakes up in the morning,

just follow him or her all day.

Ray Bradbury

I try to create sympathy for my characters, then turn the monsters loose.

Stephen King

Writers must be fair and remember even bad guys (most of them, anyway) see themselves as good—they are the heroes of their own lives. Giving them a fair chance as characters can create some interesting shades of gray— and shades of grey are also a part of life.

Stephen King

Each writer is born with a repertory company in his head. Shakespeare has perhaps twenty players ... I have ten or so, and that's a lot. As you get older, you become more skillful at casting them.

Gore Vidal

The core of every good story is a character for whom we care—and not just care a little, but care deeply. This alone is no easy task: such a character must be likable, but not annoying. He must have virtues but remain imperfect. She must possess the potential for sacrifice, for selflessness, for selfishness, for evil. He may be funny, but not only that. She may be serious, but not only that. He comprises many dimensions but not so many that he seems unreal or unpindownable.

Chuck Wendig

You have to be mean to your characters. You have to put them through bad stuff, because that's what makes a good story.

Pamela Hart

Every character has a voice, and every character a story. I stand back and let them speak their own truth.

Ambelin Kwaymullina

I was supposed to write a romantic comedy, but my characters broke up.

Ann Brashares

12
Once Around The Block

Writer's Block: When your imaginary friends stop talking to you.

Unknown

The truth is, every book is hard to write, everybody reaches a wall, whether it is a plot hole or a scene that you can't get past. So you've just go to get to the end. Even if it's not the greatest draft, if it needs rewriting, fine; at least you have a book to rewrite.

Sophie Kinsella

My block was due to two overlapping factors: laziness and lack of discipline.

Mary Garden

All writing problems are psychological problems. Blocks usually stem from the fear of being judged. If you imagine the world listening, you'll never write a line. That's why privacy is so important. You should write first drafts as if they will never be shown to anyone.

Erica Jong

We begin to judge our work too early and think we need to achieve perfection. Inevitably writer's block will come knocking because we can't meet those expectations. We need to give ourselves permission to fail so we have the freedom to explore, experiment and improve.

Lynda R Young

As soon as I stopped over-thinking my process, my infernal internal editor shut up, my characters started talking to me again, and my writing improved vastly. Turned out the very thing I thought was helping me be a good writer was holding me back.

K.M. Weiland

You will never work through writer's block if you walk away from your typewriter. That will only make it easier to walk away the next time.

James N. Frey

If you hit a wall, just keep writing. Sometimes our brains are like water pumps. We need to prime them and get through the goo before the creativity flows. Just write. You can fix it later.

Kristen Lamb

If something isn't working, if you have a story that you've built and it's blocked and you can't figure it out, take your favorite scene, or your very best idea or set-piece, and cut it. It's brutal, but sometimes inevitable.

Joss Whedon

Nothing's a better cure for writer's block than to eat ice cream right out of the carton.

Don Roff

If your characters decide to play up by going silent on you, take them for a walk. Mostly, by the time you get home they'll be chattering away to you again. Walking refreshes everything and chances are you'll be running to get back to the manuscript to continue with their story!

Kate Hamer

If you are having difficulties with a book, try the element of surprise: attack it at an hour when it isn't expecting it.

H. G. Wells

Prescription for writer's block: fear of poverty.

Peter Mayle

If you get stuck, get away from your desk. Take a walk, take a bath, go to sleep, make a pie, draw, listen to music, meditate, exercise; whatever you do, don't just stick there scowling at the problem. But don't make telephone calls or go to a party; if you do, other people's words will pour in where your lost words should be. Open a gap for them, create a space. Be patient.

Hilary Mantel

Sometimes you face difficulties not because you're doing something wrong, but because you're doing something right.

Unknown

Don't be paralyzed by the idea that you're writing a book; just write.

Isabelle Allende

Lethologica:
When you can't think of the word for
something.

Being a writer is a very peculiar sort of a job: it's always you versus a blank sheet of paper (or a blank screen) and quite often the blank piece of paper wins.

Neil Gaiman

If you tell yourself you are going to be at your desk tomorrow, you're asking your unconscious to prepare the material.

Norman Mailer

It's not the fear of writing that blocks people; it's fear of not writing well; something quite different.

Scott Berkun

Freewriting is a technique that liberates the writer from the encumbrance of correctness.

Freewriting is writing without rules, without the constraint of spelling, grammar, or even logic. To freewrite, set a goal – a number of pages, a number of words, or a period of time – and write without stopping until you reach the goal. Write without concern for quality or convention. It's a great technique for the writer who is stuck, blocked, or lost, and it's an effective warm-up exercise for any writing project.

Brian Wasko

I don't think that writer's block exists really. I think that when you're trying to do something prematurely, it just won't come. Certain subjects just need time … You've got to wait before you write about them.

Joyce Carol Oates

Many times, what people call writer's block is the confusion that happens when a writer has a great idea, but their writing skill is not up to the task of putting that idea down on paper. I think that learning the craft of writing is critical.

Pearl Cleage

If you do enough planning before you start to write, there's no way you can have writer's block. I do a complete chapter by chapter outline.

R. L. Stine

All writing is difficult. The most you can hope for is a day when it goes reasonably easily. Plumbers don't get plumber's block, and doctors don't get doctor's block; why should writers be the only profession that gives a special name to the difficulty of working, and then expects sympathy for it?

Philip Pullman

Writer's block doesn't exist…lack of imagination does.

Cyrese Covelli

Writer's Block is just an excuse by people who don't write for not writing.

Giando Sigurani

There's no writer's block; there's only distraction.

Carolyn Chute

Writer's block is just a symptom of feeling like you have nothing to say, combined with the rather weird idea that you should feel the need to say something. Why? If you have something to say, then say it. If not, enjoy the silence while it lasts. The noise will return soon enough.

Hugh Jackman

I learned to produce whether I wanted to or not. It would be easy to say oh, I have writer's block, oh, I have to wait for my muse. I don't. Chain that muse to your desk and get the job done.

Barbara Kingsolver

Do not wait to strike till the iron is hot; but make it hot by striking.

William Butler Yeats

You can't be blocked if you just keep on writing words. Any words. People who get "blocked" make the mistake of thinking they have to write good words.

Martha Grimes

13
First Draft

The first draft is just you
telling yourself the story.

Terry Pratchett

Your first draft is
your imagination's private journal.

MJ Bush

First drafts are for learning
what your novel is about.

Bernard Malamud

I'm writing a first draft and reminding myself that I'm simply shoveling sand into a box so that later I can build castles.

Shannon Hale

The function of the first draft is to help you figure out your story. The function of every draft after that is to figure out the most dramatic way to tell that story.

Darcy Pattison

Write freely and as rapidly as possible and throw the whole thing on paper. Never correct or rewrite until the whole thing is down.

John Steinbeck

I always do my draft in longhand because the ink is part of the flow.

Martin Amis

The first draft is a skeleton….just bare bones. The rest of the story comes later with revising.

Judy Blume

I expect my zero draft to be the worst writing in the history of writing thus when it turns out shockingly badly, I am unconcerned. "Why, yes, it is rubbish. No matter, that's what I was going for."

Justine Larbalestier

Half of what I write is garbage, but if I don't write it down it decomposes in my head.

Jarod Kintz

Getting the first draft finished is like pushing a peanut with your nose across a very dirty floor.

Joyce Carol Oates

Most of all, I remember: the purpose of the first draft is to figure out what story you are telling.

Darcy Pattison

You write that first draft really to see how it's going to come out.

James A. Michener

The beautiful part of writing is that you don't have to get it right the first time, unlike, say, a brain surgeon.

Robert Cormier

Writing a first draft is like groping one's way into a dark room, or overhearing a faint conversation, or telling a joke whose punchline you've forgotten. As someone said, one writes mainly to rewrite, for rewriting and revising are how one's mind comes to inhabit the material fully.

Ted Solotaroff

You do an awful lot of bad writing in order to do any good writing. Incredibly bad. I think it would be very interesting to make a collection of some of the worst writing by good writers.

William S. Burroughs

There is no limit to how rough a rough draft can be.

Unknown

Once you start writing, the book immediately loses all its shiny goodness. Instead of the theoretical perfection it was in your head, it becomes what every writer recognizes—a first draft.

Tasha Alexander

I write the first draft quickly. This is most often done in longhand. I simply fill up the pages as rapidly as I can … With the first draft it's a question of getting down the outline, the scaffolding of the story. Then on subsequent revisions I'll see to the rest of it. When I've finished the longhand draft I'll type a version of the story … When I'm typing the first draft, I'll begin to rewrite and add and delete a little then. The real work comes later, after I've done three or four drafts of the story.

Raymond Carver

I don't write easily or rapidly. My first draft usually has only a few elements worth keeping. I have to find what those are and build from them and throw out what doesn't work, or what simply is not alive.

Susan Sontag

Write freely and as rapidly as possible, and throw the whole thing on paper. Never correct or rewrite until the whole thing is down.

John Steinbeck

We all have an emotional equity in our first draft; we can't believe that it wasn't born perfect. But the odds are close to 100 percent that it wasn't.

William Zinsser

The only true creative aspect of writing is the first draft. That's when it's coming straight from your head and your heart, a direct tapping of the unconscious. The rest is donkey work. It is, however, donkey work that must be done.

Evan Hunter

Slow down and elaborate. My problem was telling too much too fast so that my first draft read more like a synopsis than a novel. Smell the flowers. Build characterization—get inside their head.

Linda Lay Shuler

The truth is, every book is hard to write, everybody reaches a wall, whether it is a plot hole or a scene that you can't get past. So you've just got to get to the end. Even if it's not the greatest draft, if it needs rewriting fine; at least you have a book to rewrite.

Sophie Kinsella

Nobody cares about your first draft. And that's the thing that you may be agonizing over, but honestly, whatever you're doing can be fixed … For now, just get the words out.

Get the story down however you can get it down, then fix it.

Neil Gaiman

The function of the first draft is to help you figure out your story. The function of every draft after that is to figure out the most dramatic way to tell that story.

Darcy Pattison

First drafts are always horrible and ugly. Don't worry about that—it's the same for everyone. Just remember that the first draft is as bad as the book is ever going to be, and if you keep redrafting, one day you will look at your horrible book and realize that you've turned it into something actually quite beautiful.

Robin Stevens

Your first draft won't be perfect, and it's damaging to think that it is. Every great book you've ever read has been rewritten a dozen times. This is the hardest thing to learn (trust me), but very, very important.

Patrick Ness

The first draft often is really fast, and I'd be terribly ashamed if anybody ever saw it.

Jonathan Dee

So in the first draft, I'm inventing people and place with a broad schematic idea of what's going to happen. In the process, of course, I discover all sorts of bigger and more substantial things.

Peter Carey

I had expected that at some point during the first draft a light would go on, and I would understand, finally, how to write a book. This never happened. The process was akin to blindly walking in the dark, feeling my way only by touch, and only recognizing dead ends when I smacked into them.

Hannah Kent

People mistakenly expect to hit the bulls-eye on the first pass. Abandon the idea that your first draft should be anything but exploration.

Gregory Ciotti

If you feel paralyzed while working on a rough draft, think of your work like a maze. Sometimes you have to write down a dead end to discover that this is NOT where the story needs to go.

Hugh Howey

Good stories are not written. They are
rewritten.

Phyllis Whitney

One of the greatest benefits of writing a truly
awful, lousy, no good first draft is that it can
only get better from there.

Martha Alderson

I don't recommend that you do major
revision during the writing of your first draft.
The temptation to stop and make major
changes is constant, and it can drive you bats.
And most of the time these changes aren't the
best thing for the story that's trying to bubble
up from your writer's mind.

James Scott Bell

Write with abandon and no constraints for
the first draft.

Francesca Lia Block

I don't write a quick draft and then revise;
instead I work slowly page by page, revising
and polishing.

Dean Koontz

Never correct or rewrite until the whole thing
is down.

John Steinbeck

I revise constantly, as I go along and then
again after I've finished a first draft. Few of
my novels contain a single sentence that
closely resembles the sentence I first set
down. I just find that I have to keep zapping
and zapping the English language until it
starts to behave in some way that vaguely
matches my intentions.

Michael Cunningham

During the first draft, lock up the internal
editor. Just write. Don't think about whether
it's good or bad. Let your fingers fly over the
keyboard and don't stop to delete.

Jody Hedlund

Don't get it right, just get it written.

James Thurber

Get it down. Take chances. It may be bad,but
it's the only way you can do anything really
good.

William Faulkner

First drafts are for learning what one's fiction wants him to say. Revision works with that knowledge to enlarge and enhance an idea, to reform it. Revision is one of the exquisite pleasures of writing.

Bernard Malamud

The easy, conversational tone of good writing comes only on the eighth rewrite.

Paul Graham

Guard your first draft with your life.

Charles Darwin

The first draft reveals the art; revision reveals the artist.

Michael Lee

Every first draft is perfect, because all a first draft has to do is exist.

Jane Smiley

Writing the last page of the first draft is the most enjoyable moment in writing. It's one of the most enjoyable moments in life, period.

Nicholas Sparks

14
Editing and Rewriting

It is perfectly okay to write garbage
as long as you edit brilliantly.

C.J. Cherry

A successful book is not made of
what is in it, but of what is left out of it.

Mark Twain

The wastepaper basket is
the writer's best friend.

Isaac Bashevis Singer

Rewriting is the crucible
where books are born.

Cathryn Louis

Revision is one of the exquisite pleasures of writing.

Bernard Malamud

Editing is like killing your story and then very slowly bringing it back to life.

Jean Oram

You write to communicate to the hearts and minds of others what's burning inside you, and we edit to let the fire show through the smoke.

Arthur Plotnik

People think that writing is writing. But actually writing is editing. Otherwise, you're just taking notes.

Caris Abani

You write your first draft with your heart and you re-write with your head. The first key to writing is to write, not to think.

Sean Connery

Rewriting is like scrubbing the basement floor with a toothbrush.

Peter Murphy

The secret to editing your work is simple: you need to become its reader instead of its writer.
Zadie Smith

A writer must have all the confidence in the world when writing the first draft and none whatsoever when editing subsequent drafts.
T. Davis Bunn

Good stories are not written. They are rewritten.
Phyllis Whitney

Writing is easy. All you have to do is cross out the wrong words.
Mark Twain

The process of rewriting is enjoyable, because you're not in that existential panic when you don't have a novel at all.
Rose Tremain

Examine every word you put on paper. You'll find a surprising number that don't serve any purpose.
William Zinsser

My rule of thumb is that a short story of 3,000

words should be rewritten down to 2,500. It's not always true, but mostly it is. You need to take out the stuff that's just sitting there and doing nothing. Always ask the student writer, "What do you want to say?" Every sentence that answers that question is part of the essay or story. Every sentence that does not needs to go.

Stephen King

Read your work aloud! This is the best advice I can give. When you read aloud you find out how much can be cut, how much is unnecessary. You hear how the story flows. And nothing teaches you as much about writing dialogue as listening to it.

Judy Blume

Writing is probably one-fifth coming up with the stuff, and four-fifths self-editing again and again and again.

David Mitchell

You come by your style by learning what to leave out.

Billy Collins

Don't look back until you've written an entire draft, just begin each day from the last

Creativity is allowing yourself to make mistakes. Art is knowing which ones to keep.

Scott Adams

If it sounds like writing, I rewrite it. Or, if proper usage gets in the way, it may have to go. I can't allow what we learned in English composition to disrupt the sound and rhythm of the narrative.

Elmore Leonard

I would advise anyone who aspires to a writing career that before developing his talent he would be wise to develop a thick hide.

Harper Lee

I notice that you use plain, simple language, short words and brief sentences. That is the way to write English—it is the modern way and the best way. Stick to it; don't let fluff and flowers and verbosity creep in. When you catch an adjective, kill it. No, I don't mean utterly, but kill most of them—then the rest will be valuable. They weaken when they are close together. They give strength when they are wide apart. An adjective habit, or a wordy, diffuse, flowery habit, once fastened upon a

person, is as hard to get rid of as any other
vice.

Mark Twain

Write until you know it's the best it could
possibly be, then give it to someone who
doesn't love you, to read. Then rewrite.

Belinda Bauer

Cross out every sentence until you come to
one you cannot do without. That is your
beginning.

Gary Provost

The best advice I can give on this is, once it's
done, to put it away until you can read it with
new eyes. When you're ready, pick it up and
read it, as if you've never read it before. If
there are things you aren't satisfied with as a
reader, go in and fix them as a writer: that's
revision.

Neil Gaiman

Generally I finish a first draft in 2-6 months,
then I set it aside for a while so that when I
come back to it I can read it with fresh eyes
and figure out how to improve it.

Margaret Haddix

Make sure your book is the best it can be. None of this "my mama liked the first draft" nonsense. Rewrite and revise until it's very good. Make it the best it can be. And don't have typos. Please, in the name of all that is good and green on this Earth, do not have typos. ESPECIALLY in your query letter!

James Dashner

Only bad writers think that their work is really good.

Anne Enright

Readers sometimes ask how much I edit my own writing. I edit until each paragraph has lost the ten pounds it gained over the winter. I edit until each sentence can survive three days in the wilderness on its own. My father taught me to look at each sentence and, if it didn't deserve to live, shoot it between the eyes. Ignore the pleas of women and children. Take no prisoners, he said.

Sy Syfransky

Read a lot. Write a lot. Delete a lot.

Hannah Richell

What lasts in the reader's mind is not the phrase but the effect the phrase created:

laughter, tears, pain, joy. If the phrase is not affecting the reader, what's it doing there? Make it do its job or cut it without mercy or remorse.

Isaac Asimov

Put down everything that comes into your head and then you're a writer. But an author is one who can judge his own stuff's worth, without pity, and destroy most of it.

Sidonie-Gabrielle Colette

A primary part of editing is trimming the fat from flabby prose. Unless you have an editor to do the job for you, you'll have to learn to do your own cutting. Prepare yourself: it will be harder than you think. Some sentences, phrases, even individual words have to be wrested from your brain. After working so hard to produce them, it can be hard to say goodbye to these little verbal darlings of ours. There's no getting around this, however. Good writing doesn't waste words. Find the core of what you want to say and scrap the rest.

Brian Wasko

I rewrote the ending to "Farewell to Arms,"

the last page of it, thirty-nine times before I
was satisfied.

Ernest Hemingway

15
Miscellaneous Thoughts

The book that will most change your life
is the book you write.

Seth Godin

It is a great privilege to make one's
living from writing sentences. The
sentence is the greatest invention of
civilization … The great thrill is when a
sentence that starts out being
completely plain suddenly begins to
sing, rising far above itself and above
any expectation I might have had for it.

John Banville

Writing, like life itself, is a voyage of discovery.

Henry Miller

Talent is helpful in writing, but guts are absolutely essential.

Jessamyn West

A writer should concern himself with whatever absorbs his fancy, stirs his heart, and unlimbers his typewriter. [A] writer has the duty to be good, not lousy; true, not false; lively, not dull; accurate, not full of error. He should tend to lift people up, not lower them down. Writers do not merely reflect and interpret life, they inform and shape life.

E. B. White

Fairy tales are more than true: not because they tell us that dragons exist, but because they tell us that dragons can be beaten.

Neil Gaiman

Writers don't have bad life days; they just have good research days.

Julie Wright

Write the book that you're desperate to read. Fall in love with your characters. Finish the day's writing at a point where you want to know what happens next. And keep writing every day.

Chelsey Pippin

You can make anything by writing.

C. S. Lewis

Writing is like a sculpture where you remove, you eliminate, in order to make the work visible. Even those pages you remove somehow remain.

Elie Wiesel

I can't imagine not writing. Writing is simply a way of life for me.

William Goyen

How vain it is to sit down to write when you have not stood up to live.

Henry David Thoreau

We are all apprentices in a craft where no one ever becomes a master.

Ernest Hemingway

The two most engaging powers of an author

are to make new things familiar and familiar
things new.

Samuel Johnson

I love writing. I love the swirl and swing of
words as they tangle with human emotions.

James Michener

I am by nature a dealer in words, and words
are the most powerful drug known to
humanity.

Rudyard Kipling

Writing, like life itself, is a voyage of
discovery.

Henry Miller

Find what causes a commotion in your heart.
Find a way to write about that.

Richard Ford

Writing to me is simply thinking through my
fingers.

Isaac Asimov

A writer needs three things: experience,
observation and imagination, any two of

which, at times any one of which, can supply
the lack of the others.

William Faulkner

Writing gives me great feelings of pleasure.
There's a marvelous sense of mastery that
comes with writing a sentence that sounds
exactly as you want it to. It's like trying to
write a song, making tiny tweaks, reading it
out loud, shifting things to make it sound a
certain way.

Susan Sontag

Either write something worth reading or do
something worth writing.

Benjamin Franklin

As a writer you try to listen to what others
aren't saying … and write about the silence.

N. R. Hart

Every secret of a writer's soul, every
experience of his life, every quality of his
mind, is written large in his works.

Virginia Woolf

The first person you should think of pleasing,
in writing a book, is yourself. If you can
amuse yourself for the length of time it takes

to write a book, the publisher and the readers can and will come later.

Patricia Highsmith

Don't confuse reading books on the craft of writing with the act of writing. You must write. And while it's essential to learn the craft, in the end you must write your own story in your own voice.

Sean Chercover

I know I was writing stories when I was five. I don't know what I did before that. Just loafed, I suppose.

P. G. Wodehouse

And now that you don't have to be perfect, you can be good.

John Steinbeck

The writer must be in it. He can't be to one side of it, ever. He has to be endangered by it. His own attitudes have to be tested in it. The best work that anybody ever writes is the work that is on the verge of embarrassing him, always.

Arthur Miller

I know nothing in the world that has as much power as a word. Sometimes I write one, and I look at it, until it begins to shine.

Emily Dickinson

Writing to me is simply thinking through my fingers.

Isaac Asimov

People may forget the plot of a beloved book, they may forget many of its scenes and characters, but people will never forget how it made them feel or the lessons it taught them.

Ana-Carolina Pereira

My favorite part about being a writer is being totally lost inside a story, so immersed that your fictional life overtakes your real one. I love the madness of that, when the story is pouring out and you feel this crazy urgency to get it down before you lose it. It's totally euphoric, and yes, completely wacko.

Jandy Nelson

The book is a snapshot of who you were at one point in time. You can't change it. It's who you are.

Lee Child

Stories never really end … even if the books
like to pretend they do. Stories always go on.
They don't end on the last page, any more
than they begin on the first page.

Cornelia Funke

Always go with the choice that scares you the
most, because that's the one that is going to
help you grow.

Caroline Myss

Every book is three books, after all; the one
the writer intended, the one the reader
expected, and the one that casts its shadow
when the first two meet by moonlight.

John W. Ford

Put it before them briefly so they will read it,
clearly so they will appreciate it, picturesquely
so they will remember it, and above all,
accurately so they will be guided by its light.

Joseph Pulitzer

A short story is a different thing altogether – a
short story is like a quick kiss in the dark from
a stranger.

Stephen King

Writing, after all, is an act of faith. We must

believe, without the slightest evidence that believing will get us anywhere.

Dani Shapiro

One always has a better book in one's mind than one can manage to get onto paper.

Michael Cunningham

A good novel tells us the truth about its hero; but a bad novel tells us the truth about its author.

G.K. Chesterton

Normally, in anything I do, I'm fairly miserable. I do it, and I get grumpy because there is a huge, vast gulf, this aching disparity, between the platonic ideal of the project that was living in my head, and the small, sad, wizened, shaking, squeaking thing that I actually produce.

Neil Gaiman

I have spent a good many years since—too many, I think—being ashamed about what I write. I think I was forty before I realized that almost every writer of fiction or poetry who has ever published a line has been accused by someone of wasting his or her God-given talent. If you write (or paint or dance or sculpt or sing, I suppose), someone will try to make you feel lousy about it, that's all.

Stephen King

Writers don't write from experience, although many are hesitant to admit that they don't. If you wrote from experience, you'd get maybe one book, maybe three poems. Writers write from empathy.

Nikki Giovanni

You must write for yourself and not what you think people want to read.

Jodi Ellen Malpas

The secret of being a writer: not to expect others to value what you've done as you value it, not to expect anyone else to perceive in it the emotions you have invested in it. Once this is understood, all will be well.

Joyce Carol Oates

I think that everything you do helps you to write if you're a writer. Adversity and success both contribute largely to making you what you are. If you don't experience either one of those, you're being deprived of something.

Shelby Foote

Writing, like life itself, is a voyage of discovery.

Henry Miller

You're learning to write a book every time you sit down to do it. I know that sounds a little strange, but in every book you're presented with new possibilities, new environment, different people, new story lines. You're learning how to do it all over again.

Carol O'Connell

The job of the artist is always to deepen the mystery.

Francis Bacon

A novel is like a bow, and the violin that produces the sound is the reader's soul.

Stendhal

The best work that anybody ever writes is the work that is on the verge of embarrassing him, always.

Arthur Miller

Words—so innocent and powerless as they are, as standing in a dictionary, how potent for good and evil they become in the hands of

one who knows how to combine them.
Nathaniel Hawthorne

My books are water; those of the great
geniuses is wine. Everybody drinks water.
Mark Twain

Being a writer is a very peculiar sort of a job:
it's always you versus a blank sheet of paper
(or a blank screen) and quite often the blank
piece of paper wins.
Neil Gaiman

Marry somebody you love and who thinks
you being a writer's a good idea.
Richard Ford

You have to write the book that wants to be
written, and if the book will be too difficult
for grown-ups, then you write it for children.
Madeleine L'Engle

Writing is turning one's worst moments into
money.
J. P. Donleavy

A little talent is a good thing to have if you
want to be a writer. But the only real

requirement is the ability to remember every scar.

Stephen King

Fiction writing is a strange business when you think about it. You sit down and weave a network of lies to explore deeper truths.

Wally Lamb

Writing's funny. It's like walking down a hall in the dark looking for the light switch, and suddenly you find it, flip it on, and then you discover the hallway you passed through is papered with the novel you've written.

Jonathan Safran Foer

There are three rules for writing a novel. Unfortunately, no one knows what they are.

W. Somerset Maugham

Writing has laws of perspective, of light and shade just as painting does, or music. If you are born knowing them, fine. If not, learn them. Then rearrange the rules to suit yourself.

Truman Capote

If the writing is honest, it cannot be separated from the person who wrote it.

Tennessee Williams

223

And finally,
Richard Brautigan once wrote,

"I always wanted to write a book that
ended with the word 'mayonnaise.'"

Other Books by Rocky Henriques

Please visit
http://amzn.to/2hlGsoZ

About The Author

Rocky Henriques has pastored churches in Mississippi since 1979. He earned a Master of Divinity degree and a Doctor of Ministry degree from New Orleans Baptist Theological Seminary. Rocky has two adult children, Jennifer and Jonathan, and two grandchildren, Emma Claire and Joshua. He lives in Mississippi with his beautiful wife Sharon, a rowdy parrot named Kermit, and two spoiled dogs, Emmy and Gabi.